I0101916

Reasonable Doubt

Exposing the Miscarriage of Justice in the Wrongful Conviction of Paul Krauss

By Jean F. Kallberg Krauss

REASONABLE DOUBT
EXPOSING THE MISCARRIAGE OF JUSTICE IN THE WRONGFUL
CONVICTION OF PAUL KRAUSS

Copyright Jean F. Kallberg Krauss, 2018

All rights reserved. Except for brief passages quoted in newspaper, magazine, radio, television or online reviews, no portion of this book may be reproduced, distributed, or transmitted in any form by any means, electronic or mechanical, including photocopying, recording, or information storage or retrieval system, without the prior written permission of the author.

ISBN 978-0-692-07641-5

Cover design by Calla Jenkinson

Manufactured in the United States of America
First printing February 2018

Dedication

My thanks first to God who brought me through this ordeal stronger in my faith.

To my amazing Bible Study lady friends at Bethel Lutheran who gave me unconditional love early on. To those three women, Linda, Jane and Bonnie who agreed to form our writers' group and encouraged me to open my heart to the pain and put it in writing, to our "gent" Aethan, who traveled with me keeping my focus on why I was writing this, and to my two best, long-term friends Helga and Theresa, who understood and supported me, my heartfelt and copious gratitude. You are all the best.

Many thanks to my multi-talented granddaughter Calla for the great cover design.

Preface

The events that lead to this book being written are difficult to recount but must be told if the reader is to fully understand the effect they have had on the lives of my family. It is, then, with tears in my eyes, that I list the six criminal charges brought against my son, Paul Krauss, in June 2006. At his two-day trial in March 2007, he was found guilty of five of them and was eventually sentenced to a total of twenty-four years in prison. The charges were based on allegations brought against Paul by the woman that he was married to at the time, his second wife.

The Charges, Verdicts, and Sentences include:

- 2nd degree Sexual Assault/Use of Force, Class C Felony; Guilty, 18 years.
- Burglary-Building or Dwelling, Class F Felony, Not Guilty
- 2nd Degree Recklessly Endangering Safety, Class G Felony, Guilty, 3 years
- False Imprisonment, Class H Felony, Guilty, 3 years
- Knowingly Violate a Domestic Abuse Injunction, Class U Misdemeanor, Guilty, 9 months
- Bail Jumping-Misdemeanor, Class A, Guilty, 9 months

It should be noted that except in the case of the two misdemeanors, the various sentences were made to run consecutively, meaning that the most severe would be served first, followed by the next most, and then the next most. It is customary to set sentences for multiple charges arising out of the same "event" concurrently, meaning that while serving the most severe, the person would also be earning "credit" toward all the other charges. In Paul's case, he would have to serve a total of 18 years, not the accumulated 24. It also should be noted that in addition to serving time in prison, a total of 13 years Extended Supervision will follow Paul's eventual release.

"It's important that we share our experiences with other people.
Your story will heal you and your story will heal someone else.
When you tell your story, you free yourself and give other
people permission to acknowledge their own story."
~ Iyanla Vanzant

PART I. LORD, YOU GAVE ME A MOUNTAIN

The true story of a mother's love for her son, and her determination to see him set free, exonerated of the charges which resulted in his being sentenced to prison for 24 years.

Prologue

An early morning phone call on Friday, June 2, 2006, from my oldest grandson, Dylan Krauss, suddenly and unexpectedly dropped the bottom out of my world. Life took a dramatic turn, not for the good. The events that started that day have affected the lives of my entire family ever since. Within a week, my son, Paul, was taken into custody, charged with four felonies and two misdemeanors, and bound over for trial. The charges were based on allegations brought by Paul's estranged wife, Melanie. The veracity of her statements, her reliability as a witness, her character, and her past history were never investigated or questioned by authorities.

During the past few years, I have researched Paul's case files and have concluded that there are four major issues that could be the bases for reopening his case and exonerating him. Each of these issues is substantiated by various court and other documents in Paul's case file.

The following issues are addressed in more detail in the second part of this book, entitled "Paul's Key":

1. Violation of Civil Rights
2. Ineffectual Assistance of Counsel,
3. Arranged/Falsified/Misrepresented/Untested Evidence
4. False and Contradictory Statements by the Accuser and Law Enforcement Officers

I have constructed this book as a two-part narrative. Part One is titled, *Lord, You Gave Me a Mountain*. Its source and significance is explained in Chapter 21. Since June 2006, I have been clawing my way up a virtual mountain, enduring the extreme burden, anguish, heartache and agony of the challenge to get justice for my son, Paul Krauss. At times, despair, helplessness, hopelessness and anxiety overwhelms me as I meet obstacle after obstacle in my efforts to find that justice. With his earliest possible release date set for 2030, I may not live to see him free at the top of that mountain. I will be ninety when he becomes eligible for release.

Part Two is titled, *Paul's Key*. It refers to the hope that the documents referred to and the explanations contained therein can be read and understood by someone who will realize the injustice that my son and our entire family has suffered at the hands of the Pierce County, Wisconsin, legal system. With that understanding, we hope a person will step forward and use this material as the basis for reopening Paul's case. That person, thus, will be "Paul's Key" to unlock the prison doors and allow him to walk out, a free man, to return to his family, especially his two sons. It is interesting to note that the Apostle Paul, who also spent time in prison, is represented by a key in liturgical symbolism.

In recounting the particular events that I personally experienced, it might seem that I have placed too much focus on myself and what I consider to be my ordeal of the years since 2006. However, I had no intention of diminishing what other family members have dealt with in these intervening years while one member has been absent from our circle. In addition, no one can ever fully appreciate or understand the horrible life that Paul himself has had to live isolated from those who love him.

I cannot adequately describe the heart-ripping, gut-wrenching, mind-numbing sorrow that crushes me at unexpected moments. I grieve Paul's loss of the everyday living, the special events, and the family gatherings. Only someone who has been through such a waking nightmare can understand the distress it causes to family members of an inmate, and the long-lasting negative effects on the children of the family.

Chapter 1

This is my story leading up to and following June 2006. I cannot speak for other members of my family about how one terrible day that month changed their lives. I recount only what life has been like for me. The tears I have cried could fill an ocean, and are always just below the surface ready to flow at the least mention of words like "home" and hearing songs like "There's No Place Like Home for the Holidays." These are reminders of how much I long for my son to be back with his two sons and the rest of his family.

My story starts years prior to that life-changing day to help the reader better understand what happened. I offer this not as an excuse for things but as an explanation.

Paul was born on December 2, 1966, the second son, of Rolland H. (Rollie) Krauss and me. Following the birth of our first child, Sean, a second pregnancy had ended in an unexpected miscarriage at three months. Paul was born just a year later. That affected the course of our family life, although at the time its significance could not be anticipated. While twenty months younger, Paul was often mistaken as a twin of his older brother because of his size, and that too, had a long-term effect on him. Others expected abilities from him before he was capable of them. He was often encouraged by his father and grandfather to "wrestle" with his older brother. While Paul weighed more than Sean, Sean was more agile. These occasions regularly ended with one of the boys in tears, usually Paul. This fostered a life-long competitive spirit between them.

Paul became our middle child when his sister, Tracey,

was born in 1968. We could not foresee the effect this would have as Paul took on the role of protector to Tracey, a role he continued to fill even later in their lives.

When Paul was about two years old, we had been tent camping with his dad's parents one weekend. When we returned home, while giving Paul and Sean their baths, I noticed a lump on one of Paul's ears. I wondered what had caused that. Knowing his dad and his grandmother had allergies, I called our family doctor. The doctor diagnosed the lump as an allergic reaction, and prescribed Benadryl, an anti-allergen. Over the next several years, I kept Benadryl on hand to use any time I noticed Paul having an allergic reaction.

By the time Paul was in third grade, his allergies had become constant irritations, and he finally was referred to an allergy specialist. On Halloween, Paul underwent multiple tests. The results indicated he was allergic to virtually all animals, household dust, one food, various grasses and plants, and every common tree except oak. Since we lived in the country outside Ellsworth, Wisconsin, we were surrounded by fields, trees and wild grasses, and had a variety of animals, including dogs, cats, rabbits, horses, chickens, several raccoons, and even a goat, at various times. Paul was living in an extremely toxic environment. He could not get away from those things that he was allergic to, whether in the house or outside. Paul felt miserable, exposed year around to multiple allergens. In spite of his runny nose and irritated eyes, he somehow managed to maintain a pretty happy demeanor.

For the next eight years, Paul was on a regimen of regular allergy shots to desensitize him. Each year, he and his dad traveled to the Twin Cities of Minnesota to see his allergist to begin new shots for the next series of allergies to be addressed. Still, he managed to maintain a pretty cheerful attitude throughout.

In addition to the allergies, Paul somehow became our bad luck child. If anything bad was going to happen to any of the three kids, Paul was usually the one it happened to. It included breaking his leg during gym class in sixth grade, chipping a front tooth in a fall, slicing the side of his knee on a piece of sharp tin requiring stitches, and a variety of other mishaps. He also had surgery to remove badly enlarged tonsils caused by the constant irritations his body had tried to fight.

Other factors in Paul's life that affected him significantly included his dad becoming a part-time volunteer deputy for the Sheriff of Pierce County, in addition to his full-time job with 3M Company working three rotating shifts. This meant that Paul's father was frequently absent during Paul's formative years. I had returned to teaching in 1969, when Paul's sister was just one year old. Those early years for Paul from age three until he started school included being under the care of a babysitter. At times, he even took care of his sister while their dad slept when on the midnight shift.

Because I was teaching in the school system our kids attended, it wasn't long before their classmates realized that our three would be having their mother as a teacher when they entered seventh grade at Ellsworth Junior High. Like the children of ministers and policemen, our kids had to endure teasing about either being "goody-goodies" or would take on the alternative of being "baddies." I was not fully aware of what this meant to each of the three kids at the time. There were a few hints along the way, but the full impact of this was only realized much later in their school years and beyond.

Chapter 2

From the time Paul turned sixteen, he worked at various jobs, and was self-sufficient and gainfully employed until his arrest in 2006. While in high school, he had several minor run-ins with the law but nothing more serious than many kids that age become involved in.

However, Paul had begun drinking, and during April 1986 spent two weeks in a rehabilitation center, followed by two weeks as an outpatient. It was the opinion of the staff there that Paul was an "alcohol abuser." This term refers to the use of alcohol to extremes with no addiction to alcohol. People with this condition are not addicted to drinking (alcoholics), but when they do drink, they over-imbibe. Typically, after a session of binge drinking, they awake in a perfectly normal state, with no aftereffects. Unfortunately, his drinking did not stop, and contributed to problems he had later in his adult life.

Paul was not one who conformed to the usual ways of society; his self-acclaimed motto became, "If you are not walking on the edge, you are taking up too much space." He became our "wild child," and eventually acquired a Harley Davidson motorcycle, his pride and joy next to his two sons.

Between his junior and senior years of high school, Paul enlisted in the United States Army Reserves. He took the first part of his basic training that summer, and completed training the summer after graduation. He served as a member of the 652nd (which soon became the 327th) Bridge Company from February 1984-February

1992. Regular meetings were held throughout that time, and summers took him to camp for several weeks. By the time he left the military, he had attained the rank of SP4 (Specialist 4).

Following high school graduation in 1985, Paul enrolled in the Industrial Machine Mechanics course offered at Red Wing (Minnesota) Technical College. He has natural abilities in a variety of mechanical and repair work, and with his special training, put them to use in the jobs he subsequently held.

Paul's drinking problems continued to escalate, and finally resulted in his losing his driving privileges, which in turn, finally opened his eyes to his drinking problem. By 1992, once and for all, Paul sobered up, stayed away from alcohol, and never drank again.

In the early 1990s, Paul was initiated as a Master Mason into Hancock Lodge #227, Ellsworth. Soon after that, he became a member of the Scottish Rite Masons. He was a Shriner with Zor Temple, Madison, Wisconsin, as well as with the St. Croix Valley Shrine Club on a local level.

Because Paul has the highly desired type AB blood, he became a donor of both blood and blood plasma throughout his adult life. As an inmate, he is no longer allowed to contribute this important service, however.

Further civic activities from 1993-2005 saw him volunteering his time and help to the truck pull at the Pierce County Fair, assisting in hooking trucks to the pulling sled. This meant hooking two weighted sleds, each to their own parallel trucks, ensuring pulls were done safely, efficiently, and in a timely fashion. Often this meant hooking 140 trucks each night.

Paul volunteered at Hillcrest Elementary School, Ellsworth, in 1998-99 with his son Dylan's kindergarten class. In the 2000s, he was a Cub Scout Leader for Dylan's Scout Pack. From 2003-2005, he was an assistant football coach for his sons' football teams with the Ellsworth Community League.

In the years from 2001-2003, he was the assistant director, then director, of the Harley Owners Group (H.O.G.) for the River Falls, Wisconsin, Harley-Davidson dealership.

From his very early years, Paul became known for his generous concern for others. I have mentioned his particular closeness to his younger sister. This sibling relationship showed itself throughout their growing-up years and continued into their young adult years as well. One touching story that illustrates the closeness between Paul and Tracey occurred when Paul broke his leg at school during sixth grade. I was called to come to the school that both kids attended, not only to be with Paul while he was taken care of by the doctor, but because Tracey had become upset and was in tears after she learned that Paul had been hurt.

One comment that I frequently have made regarding Paul is that "he would not only give you the shirt off his back, but he'd give you both his right and his left arm, if you needed them." He seemed to go out of his way to help people, including strangers, wherever he saw a need. He told me of coming upon an accident one time, and how he had done what he could to help the injured people.

In 2006, while in jail awaiting trial and sentencing, Paul helped two men get their G.E.D's (General Education Diplomas), and was put in charge of the library and rec room in the Pepin County Jail, Durand, Wisconsin. Evidently, those in charge felt he had a gift for helping others without any thought of compensation.

With his history of helping others as a stand-up kind of person from 1966-2006, it is difficult to understand how the unfounded statements of one woman could cause so much damage. She was supported by the district attorney who, we feel, had a personal motive/agenda. These two people, who barely knew him, undermined the view of Paul's character as seen by others who had known him much longer.

Chapter 3

Paul is well-known for his clever sense of humor, and over the years attracted many friends, both male and female. Because his high school and technical school years included his drinking years, his relationships with others, especially female friends, tended to be rocky and some ended in dramatic ways. He brought home several young women to introduce to us, but none of them became more than passing episodes in Paul's life. Then he met Becky in 1988, and they soon moved in together in Inver Grove Heights, Minnesota.

Their early days as a couple prior to Paul's sobriety, involved much time spent in local bars. By the time Rollie and I had our twenty-fifth anniversary in 1989, Paul and Becky were engaged, and a year later, in September 1990, Paul married Rebecka (Becky) Lea Strom.

The marriage was stormy from the beginning. During the years from 1990-1993, Becky moved out or forced Paul to move out on several occasions. But by May 1993, when their first child, Dylan, was born, they were together, living in Ellsworth.

Whether for their new baby's sake or not, Paul and Becky managed to remain together for a while. Paul had quit drinking by 1992, but Becky still enjoyed it. That certainly contributed to the problems experienced in their marriage when Paul realized they did not have much else in common. By late fall 1995, they separated and later divorced, in spite of expecting their second child. Austin was born in February 1996, and along with his older brother, began a life of alternately living one week with their mother and one week with their father.

After moving out of the home he had rented with Becky, Paul briefly stayed with his dad and me before finding another rental. He lived there for a short time before he and the two boys moved in with the woman he had become involved with prior to his final separation and divorce from Becky. Ironically, Gwen also had a son named Dylan, the same age as Paul's son. At the time, I remember jokingly referring to the possibility of the three boys forming a law firm, Dylan, Dylan, and Austin. Little did I know how the law would figure so critically in the future of Paul, his sons, and our family.

When the relationship between Paul and Gwen ended in 1998, Rollie and I co-signed on a loan for Paul as a down payment on a two-story house in Ellsworth, Wisconsin. Several generations of the Krauss family had lived in the area since the mid-1850s. Paul and the two boys lived there from about 1998-2003.

Chapter 4

Paul held a succession of jobs; each brought him better pay and added to his skills in a variety of work situations. As he had done in his school years, Paul continued to meet women, occasionally introducing some to us. None of these resulted in long-term relationships.

He met Melanie Mae Miller in March 2003. She was twenty-six years old, eleven years younger than Paul. Melanie had a daughter, Savannah, the child of her first marriage, which had ended in divorce. Savannah is the same age as Paul's younger son, Austin. Melanie had full custody of Savannah, and retained custody throughout the entire time of her involvement with Paul.

Melanie had a second daughter, Makayla, her child by a second husband, to whom she was still married, although separated, at the time she met Paul. Melanie's husband subsequently divorced her, and was given custody of Makayla. Melanie had short-term visitation rights, including some weekends.

Paul had spent a couple of brief times in jail as the result of driving after his driver's license was suspended. Because he lost jobs during these times, he was unable to keep up payments on the house he was buying, and it went into foreclosure. When he and Melanie and their children, decided to move in together, they found a rental in the country just west of Ellsworth. Paul had retained possession of furniture he and Gwen had purchased and took it with him to the new place.

On three occasions between July 2003 and December

2004, Melanie packed up her two daughters and herself, and moved out, only to eventually return each time. In May 2004, when their landlord decided to tear down the rental mobile home, Melanie purchased a house where the combined family could live. It was easier for her rather than Paul to secure a home loan as a single unmarried mother. Melanie worked at a title company and had some "connections" for securing a loan.

A small, split-entry house with a partially-finished basement met their needs. The house was ten miles south of the Village of Ellsworth, near Hager City, Pierce County, not far from the Minnesota border. The location of the house plays a large part in the events of June 2, 2006, and of the two years preceding that terrible day.

Chapter 5

On December 1, 2004, the day before Paul's thirty-eighth birthday, Paul and Melanie were quietly married in the courthouse in Hudson, St. Croix County, Wisconsin. We learned they had married only afterwards. However, from March to August 2005, Melanie and her two daughters moved out, leaving Paul in the house she was purchasing. During her several times out of the house, Melanie lived with her sister and brother, filed for a restraining order against Paul and for divorce. Meanwhile, Paul continued to make the payments on the house and paid the utilities, as well, even though everything was in her name. Perhaps this was an indication of Paul's trust and naivety in his relationship with Melanie.

Paul was her third husband between 1995 and 2004. Shortly after Paul's arrest, and before she and Paul were divorced, Melanie moved in with a man from Minnesota. This was in spite of the fact that she had voiced her "fear of men" as a result of what she claimed had occurred on that day in June 2006. When that new man "caught" her in a compromising situation with another man, she moved in with the "newer" man, later was married to him, and then divorced from him by mutual consent. It is interesting to note that on October 3, 2015, at age 38, Melanie married for the fifth time to a man, Todd Wright, aged 53, as indicated in a marriage license issued on that date in Olmstead County, Minnesota. The current status of that marriage is not known at the time of this writing.

She spent much on herself and her daughters and

adding to the financial difficulties that resulted. Paul has told me this was a continuing source of arguments during the years they were together, before and after their marriage. Melanie's birthday is in April, and there is a pattern in the years she and Paul were together of her becoming "restless" in March each year. It was often in March that she would move out. It was March of 2006 that the final break-up between Paul and her was initiated.

In August 2005, when she moved back in for the final time, Melanie dropped both the most recent restraining order and the divorce procedure. In September 2005, Paul and Melanie refinanced the house, and in Paul's words, Melanie told him he would be "on the house." He took that to mean it would be in both their names, even though he had not signed any paperwork. It was only later in 2006 that Paul came to realize this was not the case. Melanie subsequently lost the house to foreclosure because she failed to keep up the payments despite orders to do so in their temporary divorce papers.

From August 2005-March 2006, all appeared to be well. Melanie made the claim that Paul, Dylan, and Austin were "her family and she wanted the marriage to work." From what Paul has told me, Melanie returned in August only after she found out that a young woman Paul had been seeing was killed in an accident on August 24, 2005.

On Christmas Day 2005, our family was invited to the home where Paul and Melanie, now married, and supposedly reconciled, lived. It seemed to go well, and we all enjoyed the day. It was the last Christmas we would spend together as a complete family. We had no idea or warning of what would occur less than three months later, nor of the devastating day six months later when our family would be torn apart.

From February 2-6, 2006, Melanie asked me to take care of Savannah before school, to drive her to school, and to pick her up after school. Melanie would then pick Savannah up when she returned from her job each day. Melanie's usual routine included taking Savannah to the home of Paul's former wife, Becky, where Becky would put her on a bus for school. Savannah would return to Becky's after school to await her mother.

Following Paul and Becky's divorce in 1996, Becky had eventually remarried, and had two daughters with her new husband. By the 2005-6 school year, Becky was running a daycare in her new home outside of Ellsworth in an area called Beldenville. In February 2006, Becky, her new husband, and their combined family were on a trip to Florida, so Melanie had to make other temporary arrangements for Savannah to get to school that week.

On one of the days, I received a call from the school letting me know that Savannah was not feeling well, and I needed to pick her up. I took care of her for the rest of that day. When Melanie came to get Savannah on that Friday, she gave me a thank you card with a $25 gift card enclosed. I had not expected that as I considered Savannah to be my "grandchild," but I appreciated the thought and the gift.

Chapter 6

In the files I have from Paul's possessions and court proceedings is a printed Valentine card from 2006 from Melanie to Paul with a handwritten note telling him how she can "hardly wait to see him after work that evening."

Because of the shared custody between Paul and Becky, it happened that Austin's birthday in 2006 fell on the week he and his brother were at their mother's house. Austin's birthday is Feb. 15. Again, that is significant for what occurred in the next couple of weeks.

With the wintery weather normal in February in Wisconsin, it had become customary to celebrate Austin's birthdays at some fast-food restaurant where there was an indoor play area for the kids. However, because Paul and Melanie had a fairly spacious basement in their house, Paul had planned to have Austin's party there the first weekend in March.

Unbeknownst to Paul, Melanie had again secured a restraining order and started divorce proceedings against him. On March 1, Ash Wednesday, I called to talk to Paul. When Melanie answered, she told me, "He took the Durango and drove over to Red Wing."

During the hours that night and early morning, I learned that Melanie had again told Paul that she wanted a divorce. They had argued, and Paul had left, driving away in Melanie's Durango. We learned that she had called 911, telling the officer at the Pierce County Sheriff's Office Paul had a gun, and had threatened to kill her and commit suicide. He had driven the couple of miles to Red

Wing, Minnesota, where he was stopped by the local police. The vehicle was searched with no weapon being found. He was taken to the Red Wing Police station, interviewed, and released.

When Paul drove back into Wisconsin, he was again stopped, this time by Pierce County Sheriff's deputies. He was taken to their office in Ellsworth, and later transported to the Mendota Mental Health facility near Madison, Wisconsin, a four-to-five hour drive.

My husband and I learned all this when we received a late-night phone call from Paul asking us to pick him up. He was allowed to come home after having been evaluated by the personnel at Mendota as not being suicidal. The Pierce County Sheriff's Department claimed they were not responsible for bringing Paul home because they had released him from their custody, and refused to go back and get him. So my husband and I made the long, late night drive to the Madison area. Paul drove us back to Ellsworth. On my way to work the following morning, probably due to being sleep-deprived and upset, I hit a deer, damaging the front-end of the Jeep Cherokee I was driving at that time.

Chapter 7

I have mentioned that Paul's live-by motto has been, "If you aren't living on the edge, you are taking up too much space." This expresses his desire to push the boundaries of conventional expectations for living, a risky, and attention-seeking life style. For many years, he was able to "live on the edge" without too much trouble, only slipping a little from time to time but always being able to grab onto something and get back up on top again. In the couple of months before Paul took that last step, he continued to live on the edge, relying on his luck alone to keep things under control.

There are two places I am reminded of when I look back at the years between when Paul was sixteen until things began to fall apart in his life. One of these places is Stone Mountain, near Atlanta. The other is Barn Bluff, a rocky cliff that is the first thing you see driving from Wisconsin into Red Wing. Hundreds of miles apart, these two geologic formations have things in common. Both have attracted people to climb them, and they are similar in shape.

Their rounded tops are deceptive to anyone who climbs them and seeks to "get a better view" of the surrounding scenic areas. Walking away from the top-most point, the slope gradually increases until gravity takes over. Eventually the curvature becomes too great. Imagine walking on a large ball. You begin to slide uncontrollably. If you cannot grab something, you are in great danger. People have been seriously injured or lost their lives at both locations over the years.

There is a difference between "living on the edge," and going down a slippery slope. Between March 1 and June 2, 2006, Paul's slippery slope quickly increased until he began his unstoppable slide, hitting rock bottom. Our family has since felt the effects. I weep, sick at heart, each time I think about the personal and family losses we have all endured since that day.

Chapter 8

In March 2006, after being barred by her most recent restraining order from returning to the house in Hager City, Paul moved in with us for a few weeks. During that time, he was able to find a double-wide mobile home with an attached garage to rent on Pond Street in Ellsworth.

An agreement between Melanie and Paul, arranged by their lawyers, allowed Paul to retrieve his belongings from the Hager City house. Between March 18-20, Paul, his dad and I, and several friends made a number of trips transporting furniture and personal possessions to the place in Ellsworth.

On April 1, Paul, his dad and I again returned to remove what remained. Melanie took objection to items Paul was claiming, and began throwing things at Paul. She called the Pierce County Sheriff's office for an officer to be sent. Todd Hines, a deputy, responded. Upon his arrival, Melanie told him her sister, Angela, had been there all morning. However, since Paul, his dad, and I were there when Angela arrived, Rollie called that to the attention of Hines. Paul's attorney had informed him he could take what he felt was his property, and that any dispute between Melanie and Paul could be sorted out during the final divorce proceedings. Officer Hines stayed for a short time, advising us to leave with what we had already loaded up of Paul's things.

I thought that would be the last time Paul would return to the Hager City house. Little did I know it was not, and that the relationship between Paul and Melanie continued.

Later, I found out that, despite the restraining order, Paul did return on four occasions, each time at Melanie's invitation. And on at least one other occasion, Melanie came to Paul's at his invitation, and stayed there overnight, leaving behind personal items. These included her toothbrush and a newly-prescribed packet of birth control pills, with one pill removed.

Paul explained his reason for getting together with her was, "I wanted to make this marriage work. I was hoping for a reconciliation with her." I, also, believe he was looking for the approval of his father who had encouraged him to marry Melanie. Rollie's reasoning for that was to present a "proper" image to Paul's two sons, instead of Paul and Melanie just "living together."

It is significant that during the month of April 2006, Melanie chose to spend intimate time with Paul at her home and his, and it would seem, did it willingly, feeling safe doing so.

The question in my mind when I learned about the pills, became, "Why was she taking them in the first place?" I say this because, while they had been living together, and later married, Melanie expressed her wish to not have to continue taking birth control pills. Neither of them wanted to have children together. As a result of her wishes, Paul underwent a vasectomy. I knew this because I drove him to and home from the doctor's office for the procedure.

If she was only intimate with Paul, why was Melanie on birth control pills knowing it was unnecessary. She and Paul were still married. Within a month or less of forcing Paul out of the house, she was taking measures not to become pregnant.

These thoughts are mine, and did not occur to me until a couple of years later when I learned about her taking the pills. This was long after Paul was in jail. He had asked his dad to retrieve a small overnight bag from his house in Ellsworth when we had to move Paul's things while he was awaiting trial. Rollie had been instructed by Paul not to open the bag, but to simply put it away somewhere at our house for safekeeping. In 2008, when Rollie and I were preparing to move out of our house east of Ellsworth, I looked into the small bag, and discovered the pill packet with only the first pill removed.

Chapter 9

On Wednesday, May 31, 2006, Paul's sons, Dylan and Austin, were at our house in the country. Since that was Dylan's thirteenth birthday, I had invited Paul to our house after work for supper and a little birthday party for Dylan. After we ate, Paul and the boys left and drove back to their Pond Street residence.

Unbeknownst to any of us, Melanie had been in touch with the Ellsworth police the day before and had written up a complaint against Paul. Soon after Paul and the boys got home, there was a knock on the door. Paul did not answer the door but evidently one of the boys did peek out to see a police officer standing outside. We later realized the officer was there in response to Melanie's complaint.

It was customary for Paul's sons to go to their other parent's house at the end of the school day on Fridays. Since this was the week that Paul had the boys, they should have remained with him through Friday morning. I learned that Paul had asked Becky, the boys' mother, to let them instead come to her house on Thursday, June 1. It was not unusual for either parent to do some switching from time to time.

Then came that fateful phone call waking me up early on Friday morning, June 2, 2006. It was Dylan calling. "Grandma, have you talked to dad today?" The tone of his voice immediately put panic into my heart. I don't know what I was thinking, but early morning and late night calls are never good.

I don't remember getting up and dressing. The next

thing I recall, Becky, the two boys, and their two step-sisters, were at our house. Becky began by saying, "Melanie called me to say Paul broke into her house this morning. She said he had a knife and threatened her." Becky went on to relate further details that Melanie had told her. The two boys were understandably upset hearing what their mother was saying about their dad. Dylan, the older boy, was especially reacting to what she was saying.

Becky asked if she could leave the boys with us while she took the two girls to their paternal grandmother. When she came back, we talked more about what Melanie had told her. If true, the details were frightening, and worry for Paul's safety gripped me.

Over the next several days, I tried to reach Paul on his cell phone, but each time it went to voice mail. I left messages pleading with him to call me, but did not hear anything until five days later on Wednesday, June 7. Paul had been located at a motel near Wabasha, Minnesota, and had agreed to surrender to Wabasha authorities. After an interview in Wabasha, Paul was transported to Ellsworth by Pierce County officers, and jailed.

In the days between June 2 and June 7, Paul had evidently traveled to places outside of Ellsworth after hearing initial police radio messages regarding him on his scanner. Because his dad had worked with the Sheriff's Department, it became a regular part of our lives to listen to our home scanner, as well as ones carried in our family vehicles. I was not aware of Paul's whereabouts until long after he was tried and convicted. To my knowledge, he went as far east as Eau Claire, Wisconsin, and west to Wabasha.

Chapter 10

After several delays in setting dates for Paul's trial, along with different public defenders being appointed, we finally were in court in March 2007 for a two-day jury trial. I remember the weather during those two days as being typical of March, cold, rainy, windy. As I sat in the courtroom listening to the things that were being said by the district attorney and Paul's attorney, I was numb. I wanted to pinch myself to see if this was real or only a horrible dream from which I couldn't awaken. I have looked at the court transcript of those two days, and I realize how poorly Paul's attorney handled Paul's defense. I remember thinking at the time that I could have done a better job. His attorney barely objected to whatever the district attorney said, and the few times he did object, the judge refused to listen to him. It felt so one-sided, with the district attorney pompously strutting across the floor, slanting everything toward trying to show that he thought Paul was a terrible person.

I learned something about Paul's appointed attorney that I feel may have contributed to the way he conducted himself during the two days of the trial. During the lunch break on the first day, some of our family went to the Subway shop near to the courthouse. Paul's attorney asked if he could join us, as we ate. In his opening statement to the jury, Mr. Liptak had drawn the jury's attention to a bruise on his forehead, explaining that he had received it as a result of a fall down his basement stairs several days prior to the trial. As we shared lunch with him, he also told us he was a diabetic. Mr. Liptak is a very heavy-set man, and these three conditions – the head injury, diabetes, and obesity – may have caused him to not be in the best of health. This especially seemed to affect him during the second day of the trial, as we noticed him perspiring profusely, wiping his face repeatedly, and sitting in his chair for virtually the whole time that day. Did this contribute in any way toward the ultimate outcome of the trial?

As the trial drew to a close on the second day, a Friday, the jury was dismissed to do its deliberations. All too soon, it seemed, they were back with their verdicts on the six charges that had been brought against Paul. Guilty on all but one! I was in shock, as I heard this.

Paul's attorney had assured us that he had just the right "evidence" to prove Paul had not done what his accuser had described. Looking back from my vantage point all these years later, and knowing what I now know, I realize that you definitely "get what you pay for." Since we hadn't paid for a private attorney, we got attorneys that had no real personal investment in Paul's case. They would be paid by the State of Wisconsin no matter what the outcome might be. A private attorney would have been more concerned with building his reputation as a defender and would likely have put much more time and effort into preparing for trial, something that did not happen in Paul's case.

Paul was sentenced to twenty-four years in prison. Since first arrested, Paul has remained locked up, except for court appearances, transportation from one corrections facility to another, and hospital and doctor appointments while in custody.

Chapter 11

The intervening years since Paul was arrested in 2006 have brought much suffering for Paul, and great cost to my physical and spiritual well-being, my emotions, and my finances. My marriage saw significant changes. Life as I had known it previous to June 2006 ended, taking a direction I could never have imagined possible. I have learned more about the legal system than I ever hoped or wanted to know.

Many mornings, I awakened with a momentary thought that I had had a bad dream. Then, I would be hit with a heavy punch to my stomach, a cruel reminder that it was not a dream. Food no longer appealed to me. I existed on apples and sliced beef sandwiches for months. They were the only thing I could tolerate. I lost many pounds, and people began asking if I was ill. If being heartsick is considered an illness, then, yes, I was sick. I functioned like a robot; every day doing what had to be done. There were times when the horrible reality would completely overtake me, and I would break down into sobbing hysteria until exhausted.

Chapter 12

Each year since the initial life-changing event in June 2006 can be delineated by other major occurrences in my life. Since I don't live isolated from other family members, it can be assumed that each of those major things affected others as well. However, this is my account of life after June 2006, and Paul's conviction and sentencing in 2007. I can only describe what these events were, and how I dealt with them.

The year 2007 included the trial and subsequent sentencing, after two pre-sentencing investigations were done, one by the state and a private one. Paul was given a 24-year prison sentence, in spite of a lesser recommendation from the person who had done the state's pre-sentencing investigation. He was sent to Dodge Correctional Institution for evaluation and determination of the appropriate prison placement, a standard procedure.

Early in 2008, to secure the services of a private appeals attorney, we sold the property where we had lived since 1965, previously owned by several generations of the Krauss family since the 1850s. We spent weeks sorting what to keep and what to throw away, the accumulation of forty-three years living as a family. Several large dumpsters were filled and taken away. Personal property was auctioned off, and an attorney was retained. We located a rental property in the Village of Ellsworth, and a huge move from country living to "city" began. By April, we were out of the old homestead.

In 2009, the rental property was threatened with

foreclosure, and we had to choose to either move elsewhere or buy it. We decided to purchase it. That meant going into debt with the loan needed to purchase the house. We had been relatively debt-free prior to this. Taking on this huge financial burden continued to take a toll on my husband and me. We had both retired by January 2000 and felt comfortable with the life we envisioned for ourselves. Things had already begun to decline in subtle ways for my husband's health, and trying to find another rental, having to face another move, was too overwhelming to consider. So we made an offer on the house, settled on a price, and used some of the funds we had realized after the sale of the country house for a down payment. We closed on the new purchase in October 2009.

In 2010, Paul's two sons came under our guardianship when their mother abandoned them into our care one night. They lived with us for two to three years during their high school years. Their story would provide enough material for a whole book on its own. The effects of losing their dad during their growing up years cannot be calculated or fully understood. They would have to describe life without their dad themselves. Even to the present, those effects continue to weigh on them and affect the direction their lives have taken.

During that same year, my husband was diagnosed with Parkinson's disease, which affects the muscles. While the person is alive, it can only be diagnosed by the symptoms of stiffness, difficulty in walking, and shaking of the hands. Later, Rollie's neurologist diagnosed Lewy Body Dementia, often associated with Parkinson's. This disease affects the cognitive part of the brain, and makes it difficult to understand new concepts and carry out a sequence of small tasks. These are both progressive diseases with no cure.

In 2011, we purchased a Jeep Liberty to replace the faulty car Rollie was driving at the time. I became the driver of the new car, and Rollie began using the Dodge van I had been driving.

In 2012, Rollie totaled the Dodge van in an accident several blocks from our house. That was the end of Rollie driving. Austin was sixteen with a driver's license, still living with us. We purchased a used vehicle for him to drive, and to secure a slightly better rate for insurance coverage had him as the designated driver. This vehicle was later sold when Austin no longer lived in our house.

Advancing deterioration in Rollie's health became apparent by 2013. Rollie needed round-the-clock supervision and care which I could not provide. With the help of my brother, I was able to find new accommodations for Rollie. In April, he became a resident at Comforts of Home in Hudson. Several months later, I moved into a rental townhome in Hudson.

In April 2014, I slipped on ice outside my front door, fracturing my left ankle on both sides. The house in Ellsworth was still on the market, adding another stress to my already over-loaded life. By October I had an offer on the house. However, for months I dealt with the bank that held the mortgage. Since the house was valued at less than what we had paid for it, the bank was reluctant to okay the sale. Finally, I was able to close on the house in July 2014.

In November 2015, a second surgery was done to remove metal plates and other hardware from my ankle. Then in December, Rollie died.

Chapter 13

Since summer 2006 when I purchased tennis shoes for Paul to wear instead of the flip-flops furnished him while being held in the Pierce County Jail, I have continued to provide on-going financial support for him. In 2007, after he was sent to Columbia Correctional Institution in Portage, Wisconsin, I began ordering various basic "amenities" for him through state-approved vendors. Rules regarding what he could have, and how things had to be purchased kept me on a learning curve. Even today, with rules and approved vendors changing, I still make mistakes in ordering things for him.

A detailed list of the monetary costs would fill many pages, but examples include: stationery and postage for him and for me; certain clothing items and toiletries; legal fees; gas and food for visits; newspapers and magazines; copy paper and ink cartridges; typewriter and typing supplies; televisions, radios, watches.

In my files over the years are copies of nearly two hundred orders I have placed for Paul. Some are repeats for stationery, clothing items, electronics, for example, anything that gets used up or worn out. Paul is not allowed to keep broken or damaged items, has to pay to ship them to me, and I have ordered replacements. Often these things have been broken by guards while packing up his property to move him from one cell to another, or from prison to prison.

There are many "hidden" costs to the families of inmates. While it is Paul locked up, I am also locked up in a sense. I have not entirely abandoned my son to the

Department of Corrections system. Until I experienced the horror of the legal system, I never realized how the family of an inmate suffers with their incarcerated member.

Inmates are "paid" a certain amount while incarcerated, but the amount is almost laughable at a few cents an hour for an 8-hour day. If "lucky," an inmate might secure a "job" and earn a few more cents an hour. This money is "deposited" as credit in a canteen fund. The inmate can purchase certain items, such as soap, toothpaste, deodorant, and limited food items.

Occasionally, special "packages" are available, such as at Christmas. If an inmate does not have credit in his canteen fund, he cannot purchase anything. At times, therefore, I have sent money orders in his name to add to his canteen fund.

One costly item I have not yet mentioned is for telephone calls. For the first several years, Paul was able to make collect calls to my home phone. The calls were limited to 15-20 minutes each, at a cost of about $5 each time. In more recent years, collect calls are no longer available with landline phone companies, and it is necessary to have a pre-paid phone account that costs about $2 per 20-minute call. These accounts have to be set up for certain phone numbers and are able to include calls to cell phones.

Paul has always phoned me whenever away from home. I am his most dependable outside contact, so he calls me often. I accept his calls as much as possible, two or more times a week, sometimes even daily. At $2 per call, this adds up quickly, amounting to $500 or more yearly. Multiplying that by the number of years that Paul has been locked up gives a rough estimate of $5000-6000 or more.

If it seems that I have spent a great deal of time commenting about expenses, it is only because this is the only tangible thing that can be measured. The emotional, psychological, and spiritual impact on me can never truly be either measured or comprehended.

Chapter 14

While Paul was held between June 2006 and January 2008, we made numerous visits to various county jails prior to his final transfer to prison following sentencing. These included Pierce County (Ellsworth), Pepin County (Durand), and Outagamie County (Appleton). Each of these had their own visiting rules and arrangements, the worst being the Appleton jail, where he was temporarily housed awaiting an opening at one of the state prisons.

After a couple of months, Paul was transferred to Columbia Correctional Institution, Portage, Wisconsin. It was there on January 2, 2008, that we had our first visit with Paul in a prison setting, when my husband, Paul's two sons, and I drove the nearly 200-mile distance.

Beginning from when he was sent to Dodge Correctional, Paul has learned to constantly watch all around him, no matter where he might be. When we are in the visiting room with him, we notice him checking what is going on everywhere. It is a bit disconcerting for us, because he doesn't seem to be listening to us as we are telling him things. When asked about this, he simply responds, "I'm listening, but I need to keep aware of things."

After he was finally moved to Portage, I was surprised and glad that, at least there, we were finally able to greet each other with hugs, to sit beside him, and to purchase and share snacks and beverages from vending machines located in the visiting room.

Over the next several years, we came to know two of

the visiting room guards, and to feel their compassion for the situation, especially since Paul's sons were so young. One of the guards, especially, went out of his way to speak to the boys and to us. We came to appreciate "Porter."

The trip to see Paul took a total of about twelve hours from the time we left home, spent four hours visiting, and then returned home. Before driving to the prison, we usually stopped at a Dairy Queen to feed the two boys and ourselves. Sometimes we also stopped on the way home to eat a late supper before dropping the boys off with their mother. With gassing up the car before we left Ellsworth, and topping off the tank before leaving Portage, costs became significant, especially when the price of gas reached an all-time high of about four dollars a gallon. We tried to schedule visits on days when school was closed, so the boys would not accumulate unexcused absences on their records.

Chapter 15

Early in 2008, we had decided that Paul needed a private appellate attorney to determine whether or not he had a case that could be appealed. It is usual to file a request for an appeal immediately after a trial ends with a guilty verdict, and that had been done by Paul's appointed trial attorney.

A state-appointed appellate attorney met briefly with Paul early the first day we visited Paul in Portage. When we arrived for our visit, we found Paul visibly upset because, after a very short meeting with him, the attorney had advised him there was nothing to appeal. That was when we felt it was necessary to get a second opinion. We were able to come up with a retainer fee to hire an attorney to meet with Paul. The private attorney let Paul and us know that he felt there were indeed grounds for appeal, and that he would begin working on preparing the appellate brief. This necessitated coming up with a large amount of money to pay for his services.

I felt that the only way to pay the necessary fees was to put our house up for sale, which we did in March 2008. By this point, my husband had started to shut down and was detaching himself from everything that was happening with our son. It may have been at this time that Rollie was actually beginning to experience the symptoms that would later lead to a diagnosis of Parkinson's disease in 2010.

It became apparent that I would have to step forward and manage whatever the future would bring. I began looking for a rental property for the two of us to live in, and quickly found just what we needed in the form of a small, two-bedroom house in the Village of Ellsworth. It offered a nice corner location, two-car attached garage, full basement, much storage, and included appliances.

Buyers were found almost immediately for our country property, and we began the huge task of downsizing our belongings, moving into town, and preparing for an extremely large auction. Closing dates on the property were postponed several times, but by June 2008, we no longer were owners of the country place in the Town of Ellsworth but renters in the Village of Ellsworth.

Chapter 16

Paul's two sons, Dylan and Austin, lived full-time with their mother, Becky, stepfather, Jamie, and two younger half-sisters from the time of Paul's arrest in June 2006 until March 2010, when their mother brought them to our house late one night. During the four years, we had received numerous phone calls from either one or the other of the boys. These calls generally had to do with complaints and appeals to us regarding treatment they received from Jamie. At times, we picked them up, but for the most part we felt helpless to intervene on their behalf.

When we talked with the boys on our trips to see Paul, they would elaborate on certain things they said they were experiencing at Jamie's hands. In particular, they seemed to feel they were made to "earn" the right to live in the house in Beldenville that Becky and Jamie had built following their marriage sometime after Paul and Becky's divorce. Jamie drove an over-the-road semi-truck route, and often on his return home, he would order the boys to wash the truck and trailer. If it didn't pass his inspection, they were made to do it over again. There certainly is nothing wrong with young children having chores. Such things should be done to teach responsibility not to "pay for" their board and room. That kind of thing being required of young children went out long ago.

Among other things the boys related to us were how Jamie tried to enforce his demands on them, especially on Dylan. Dylan was thirteen when Paul was arrested, and by the time he came to live with us at age seventeen, he had grown into a strong young man. In those four years of being without his dad, and having another man trying to fill that vacant place in his life, Dylan began to rebel against Jamie and refused to obey him. Jamie began to use physical force to gain control over Dylan. There were several incidents the boys described that seemed to be leading toward some kind of serious conflict, with possible major consequences. One of the incidents involved a window in the front door being broken when Jamie threw Dylan against it.

Things finally came to a head when we received a call from a sobbing Dylan, asking us to come and get him because Jamie had "kicked him out" of the house. We quickly drove the couple of miles, and found Dylan standing at the end of the rather long driveway from the house. He had a duffel bag with him. When he got into our car, he was still crying. As we drove back toward Ellsworth, I asked Dylan what had happened. I don't remember the exact details, but he did show us some bruises on his arms. I told him something had to be done before things got any worse. I asked if he would go with us to the sheriff's office to tell the officers what had happened. He said he didn't want to do that, but he did agree to talk to an officer if one would come to our house.

When we arrived home, I made a call to the sheriff's office, and an officer soon arrived. He took pictures of Dylan's injuries and questioned Dylan on the details of the incident. As a result of this, an arrest order was issued for Jamie, and he was subsequently taken into custody. He spent the night in the county jail and made an appearance in court the following day. The judge released Jamie on probation and ordered him to have no-contact with Dylan for a year. It was shortly after this that Becky filed for and obtained a divorce from Jamie. She and the children moved into a house in Ellsworth where she and Paul had lived at the time Dylan was born. From then on, her daughters began the alternate week pattern of living between their parents. At some point, Becky could not continue paying the rental at that house, and moved into a mobile home in the local trailer court.

In 2016, Becky purchased a house south of the Village of Ellsworth and married for the third time. Dylan has lived with several friends since moving out of our house. Austin has been living with his mother since he finished his junior year of high school in 2012.

Chapter 17

I have said that each year, starting in 2006 when Paul was arrested, brought another major concern for us. We were barely into 2010, in March to be exact, when the next crisis hit us. We received another one of those late night, unexpected phone calls. This one came from Becky, the mother of Paul's sons. She was angry and upset as she described what was going on between her and Dylan, the oldest son. They were arguing, and she was threatening to call the police to have him removed from her house. By this time, Becky had divorced her second husband, the father of her two daughters, and she and her family were living in a trailer court in Ellsworth.

After calming her down and speaking with Dylan on the phone, we agreed that she could bring Dylan over to our house for the night, and discuss the situation in the morning. A short time later, I opened the back door to see not only Dylan, but his younger brother, Austin. I was surprised to see both boys, since I had only been expecting Dylan. When I asked Dylan what was going on, he said, "Grandma, I wouldn't leave without Austin." When I looked at Austin for some explanation, he said, "Grandma, I wouldn't stay without Dylan." The boys had decided they would stick together through whatever was to come.

The following day, instead of discussing things with us concerning the boys, Becky called Austin to tell him to be ready to go with her after school to pack up all their belongings to bring to our house. She effectively was giving her sons to us.

School was still in session when the boys came to our

house, and nothing more was done until the close of school for the summer. Realizing that Becky had no intention of reclaiming the boys, I decided that something on a legal basis was needed. After consulting with our regular attorney, we determined to seek guardianship for the boys until they reached the age of 18. Becky was approached with this proposal by our attorney, and she agreed to the plan. Paul was very agreeable to the arrangement, and on August 10, 2010, the boys were officially our wards.

Dylan was 17 and Austin was 13 when they came to live with us. Their lives had been chaotic during the intervening four years since their dad had been arrested. We had had no previous participation in raising them other than occasional short visits, and as grandparents were not as prepared as we thought we were to handle teenagers. I became the person who tried to keep discipline and order in our lives as a new family combination. My husband was less involved than he might have been due to those unforeseen, progressing illnesses that seemed to erupt during that summer of 2010. By August, he was diagnosed with Parkinson's disease, and not long after that, Dementia with Lewy Bodies was added to the diagnosis. Over the next several years, Rollie's illnesses became more and more debilitating, and more and more of the managing of our lives became my responsibility.

With two teenage boys in the house, costs rose, and though manageable, were significant. Along with that, the boys were becoming less manageable, and began acting out in various ways, including encounters with illegal activities. Fortunately, none of these earned them jail time, but by the time Dylan graduated in 2011, I had found it necessary to make him leave. At age 18, he was officially referred to as an "emancipated minor," and as such could make his own decisions about most aspects of life.

Austin continued to live with us until the end of his junior year in high school, and then moved in with his mother and two half-sisters. For the most part, I have had very little part in their lives since both boys moved out. I see them on some holidays, we have gone to visit their dad together a few times, and I get occasional phone calls and text messages from them.

Chapter 18

I n 2012, significant changes continued in our lives. It had become more and more apparent that Rollie's illnesses were becoming too problematic for him, and for me to manage. Early in the fall, my daughter-in-law, Sean's wife, who is a registered nurse, went with me to the local county office seeking assistance for Rollie and me. We did not have long-term disability insurance, and lived on our social security, Rollie's pension, and my small pension. With a great deal of time, and effort, I was able to secure government-funded aid for in-home health care for Rollie. However, because it had taken so long to get the necessary paperwork done, and due to the limited help resources available in our immediate area, it was all too apparent that the help we received came too late, and was completely insufficient to provide what was needed to take care of Rollie.

More and more frequently he was falling and unable to get up without assistance, and he was unable to do the most basic self-care functions. Things came to the point on Easter 2013 when I could no longer manage taking care of him. With the support of my family, especially my brother, I began looking for a facility that could provide Rollie with the twenty-four hour every day care and supervision he needed.

In April, after visiting several area assisted-living homes, I was able to secure a place for Rollie at Comforts of Home in Hudson. With the help of family, Rollie was moved to Hudson, I put the Ellsworth house on the market, and began searching for a place for me to move near him.

In July 2013, I moved into a two-bedroom townhome, and life calmed down to manageable proportions for me. A buyer for the Ellsworth home had come forth in October, but financial legalities kept a closing date at some future point.

I had been told that Rollie's total costs at the assisted-living facility would be fully covered through Medicare and Medicaid. Much to my shock and surprise, several months after we moved into our new separate living arrangements, I began receiving bills for his "room and board." I contacted the county agency in Pierce County where I had originally secured the assistance. After several weeks of waiting for the agent to research the issue, I learned that yes, indeed, I was responsible for paying that part of his financial debt. I began covering his monthly fees, adding what I could to each month's bill to reimburse what was owed from the time he first entered the medical care system.

Chapter 19

In late February 2014, I was invited to fly to Fort Myers, Florida, to spend a couple of days with my brother, Bill, and sister-in-law, Liz. I then traveled with them to Gainesville, Georgia, by car to spend the first weekend in March with our two sisters, Margie, whose house we stayed at, and Mary Isabelle, who drove down from Charlotte, North Carolina.

After leaving Gainesville, we spent several days driving back home through much snow and cold weather. We experienced car trouble as we neared Rockford, Illinois. We spent two nights waiting for repairs, only to be told that needed parts would be delayed. Bill and Liz procured a rental car, and we were finally on our way home. They dropped me off in Hudson before returning to Minnesota, where they live.

On Thursday, April 3, 2014, I managed to find winter's last small patch of ice right outside my front door, and slipped, breaking my left ankle in two places. After the initial shock of realizing what had just happened, I crawled back into my house, called my daughter at work a few blocks away, and was transported by ambulance to the local hospital. I stayed overnight on Thursday, had surgery to stabilize my ankle on Friday, and remained hospitalized until Sunday afternoon when it was decided that I would be discharged to my home using a wheelchair.

Tracey came several times a day at first, assisting me until I was allowed to put weight on my foot some six weeks later. The summer of 2014 was spent doing rehab using a surgical boot, a walker, and finally, a cane for stability.

I still had to deal with the house sale in Ellsworth. After much wrangling and paperwork too tedious to recall, along with several postponed closing dates, I was finally able to close on the Ellsworth property in July 2014. I remember holding my breath all the way to Ellsworth for the closing, waiting in the attorney's office for all the participants to arrive, signing the large stack of forms, walking with the attorney's assistant to the local courthouse a block away, and having to hand over the original power of attorney I held in Rollie's name. I was fearful that the original form might somehow get lost in all the immense files held in the courthouse, and directed that it not be sent back to me through the mail. I waited a couple of weeks before I received the notice that I could return to the Pierce County Courthouse and retrieve that all-important document. I breathed a huge sigh of relief when it was safely back in my hands.

It was fortunate that a couple of years earlier, we had formally completed the legal power of attorney and medical power of attorney forms while Rollie could still be considered competent to understand what the forms were, and was able to sign his own name. At the time when it became necessary for Rollie to need the extra care available at the assisted living facility, he probably might not have understood the significance of them, and possibly not been able to sign his own name. It could have proven to be an obstacle for me to manage all our affairs without that. Luckily, Rollie had agreed to make the move to Hudson after seeing the residence and discovering that one of his former 3M co-workers was also living there. With only a few comments from Rollie on occasion, we all felt that he was content with his new living arrangements, and that he was well-cared for there.

Although I was healed from my broken ankle, it continued to cause daily discomfort and affected my walking. In late October 2015, after consulting with my orthopedic surgeon, it was decided to remove the metal plate and other hardware that had been originally inserted at the time of the injury. The surgery was done just before Thanksgiving in November, and after a short time of using crutches, and then a cane for balance, I fully recovered and have been relatively pain-free since.

Chapter 20

Between 2013 and 2015, Rollie's health had continued to deteriorate, and in December of 2015, we were advised to enter him into the hospice program at Comforts of Home. Again, my daughter-in-law was with me to help me through the necessary paperwork on December 2.

About a week later, I received a call that Rollie was not eating well and had stopped taking most of the medications he had been on for so many years. On Friday, December 11, another call let me know that it might be well to gather the family together to visit Rollie as he was no longer eating, taking meds, or getting out of bed. We spent much of the day in his room with him on Friday, and the next day, Saturday, December 12. We left for a short time to attend the 5:30 p.m. worship service at Bethel Lutheran Church – Highlands, and returned to be with Rollie until about 8:30 p.m. He was resting and being kept comfortable, and we decided we had to take care of our family needs for the time being, not knowing how much time Rollie still had left. Within an hour after I got home, I had barely gotten ready for bed, and was trying to get warmed up, when I received a call telling me Rollie had died.

A phone call from me to Tracey with the news sent her to Comforts of Home to deal with whatever had to be done to start making arrangements for Rollie's funeral. The following week was spent planning the funeral, notifying friends and relatives, and arranging for a Masonic funeral service at our church, Bethel Lutheran – Highlands, in

Hudson.

With the help of family, especially daughter Tracey, daughter-in-law Dawn, and grandchildren, arrangements were made, photo displays prepared, music and refreshments selected, so that by the weekend of December 17-18, 2015, we were able to give Rollie a beautiful and touching Celebration of Life service. His cremains were taken back to Ellsworth, and were laid to rest among other family members in the cemetery owned by the church he had grown up in. St. Paul's United Church of Christ (UCC) cemetery is located just one fourth of a mile from the home place we, and several previous generations, had once owned and lived on. Rollie had come full circle back to the area where he had lived until he was 73 years old.

Chapter 21

Elvis Presley recorded a song written by Marty Robbins, a country western singer-songwriter, called "You Gave Me a Mountain." Some lines from the lyrics of that song are descriptive of what life has been like for Paul, and for me since June 2, 2006. "You know, Lord, I've been in a prison for something that I never done," is one line in particular which applies to Paul. He has maintained since the first day that he did not do the things Melanie accused him of.

"But this time, Lord, you gave me a mountain, a mountain you know I may never climb. It isn't just a hill any longer. You gave me a mountain this time." How well that describes the overwhelming feeling that hit me that day, and continues to cause me heartache and grief. In dealing with all the thousands of details and consequences resulting from the events of June 2006, it does seem that I have climbed hill after hill alone. The mountain is still ahead of me, but my faith has grown stronger over the years. I know now that God is climbing that mountain with me. That will be true until the day I see my son walk out of prison, a free man. I only hope that I will live to see that day, and that it happens soon.

PART II.
PAUL'S KEY

Introduction

H ere begins the presentation of the issues that Paul and I have determined are significant in substantiating several bases for re-opening and re-examining his case with the goal of securing his release. There are concerns regarding the handling of Paul's case beginning with his arrest on June 7, 2006. Questions arise about the ultimate verdict of guilty following his March 2007 trial, and how his subsequent sentencing and incarceration were determined.

Everything in this part is based on official documents and court records in Paul's legal case. I had first thought it would be sufficient to simply explain the significance of each document, and then include pertinent portions of it. However, those who critiqued my original manuscript suggested a far different approach. Their wisdom has prevailed, and thus a nonfiction narrative is presented making it more readable and understandable.

There are four issues to be considered. They are not presented in chronological sequence. Clarifications are given so that the reader can better understand the various arguments presented through them, and the significance of them. The official records can be found in Paul's attorneys' case file, and those held at the Pierce County Courthouse, Ellsworth, Wisconsin. Each issue will be introduced by the author's explanation of the significance of it.

Issue 1. Violation of Civil Rights

On June 7, 2006, Paul was arrested at the Wabasha

(Minnesota) Motel on a warrant issued earlier by the Pierce County (Wisconsin) Sheriff's Department. Paul was first transported to the Wabasha County Jail that day where he was read his Miranda Warning, which includes several statements. One of those statements reads, "You have the right to talk to a lawyer and have him present with you while you are being questioned." Further, "If you cannot afford to hire a lawyer, one will be appointed to represent you before any questioning, if you wish." It also states, "You can decide at any time to exercise these rights and not to answer any questions or make any statements."

A report dated June 9, 2006, by Bruce VonHaden, Investigator with the Pierce County Sheriff's Department, describes the interview he did with Paul on June 7. VonHaden writes, "I read Paul his Miranda Warning." Although he goes on to say that Paul initially said he would speak with VonHaden, he reports that after a lengthy discussion about needing an attorney or not, Paul decided he would not speak until he had time to consult an attorney, and that he wanted an attorney to come directly to the jail for the interview.

At this point the interview should have concluded. However, in his report, VonHaden says, "I did not feel this was a feasible attempt...I did not feel a local attorney would be suitable for the situation, because I did not think Paul had money to pay them for the visit."

This is the first of many illustrations of what seem to be violations of Paul's civil rights, and occurred on the very day he was arrested There is no specific written record of what exactly was said, what questions might have been asked, or what Paul may have replied in this initial interview by a Pierce County Investigator.

In his Investigative Report from June 9, VonHaden

notes that he activated his tape recorder, with the comment that, "Paul knew I did this." VonHaden claims his recording "was placed into evidence." The interview was witnessed by Wabasha County Deputy Yordie as noted on p. 2 of Von Haden's report.

On the second day of Paul's trial, Judge John Damon, the presiding judge, referred to in trial documents as The Court, commented, "I'd like to put some limits only because it's Friday afternoon and we don't want them out until 8:00." It appears that The Court is more concerned about the jury possibly having to stay late to do its deliberations than any concern about Paul's right to a fair trial.

Moments later, Paul's appointed attorney, Lester Liptak, recalls Investigator Bruce VonHaden to the stand. VonHaden is asked, "You've been sitting in court as the court officer for the district attorney during both days of this trial, correct?"

VonHaden replies, "Yes."

Question: "And you've been listening to the testimony?"

Answer: "Yes."

It is customary that anyone who is to be a witness testifying at a trial not be present in the courtroom until after they have given their testimony. The reasoning behind this is that they will not be influenced by hearing what other witnesses might say about the case before the judge and jury. I have personally been a witness on several occasions and found this to be the usual procedure. Since VonHaden is being called as a witness, and this particular testimony is recorded as having occurred on Day 2 of Paul's trial, it is quite clear that VonHaden has been present in the courtroom from the very beginning of the trial, and would have heard any testimony given during that time. This could have an adverse influence on his testimony, and possibly be another violation of Paul's right to a fair trial.

During the sentencing hearing for Paul, The Court makes comments before imposing sentence. He says, "...then we sat through a jury trial, which the only purpose I could see was to place the victim in another situation where he had opportunity to confront her. As far as listening to any defense, there...he didn't provide one to what happened and so it was just another method in my mind, I know he has the right to that process, but another method he used to try and exercise control of the situation."

In the Sixth Amendment to The Constitution of the United States of America, certain rights are guaranteed, including Speedy Trial, Public Trial, Impartial Jury, Impartiality, Venire of Juries, Sentencing, Vicinage, Notice of Accusation, Confrontation, Compulsory Process, Assistance of Counsel; Self-representation. Several of these issues are of particular concern in Paul's case, and are clearly violated by the judge himself.

Under Confrontation, there is a reference made regarding the accused having the opportunity to cross-examine the accuser. Judge Damon's comment seems to suggest that Paul only wanted to "confront her," and thus appears to be a violation of Paul's right to confront his accuser.

Judge Damon says, "As far as listening to any defense, there – he didn't provide one to what happened..." Included in the Text of the Fifth Amendment to the United States Constitution, are these words, "...nor shall be compelled in any criminal case to be a witness against himself..." Again, it would seem that Judge Damon is suggesting that "it was just another method...used to try and exercise control of the situation."

The Court continues "... he sees himself as an innocent victim." It stands to reason that if a person feels he is innocent, he would continue to maintain that stance. Paul has maintained his innocence since he was taken into custody and continues to do so through the present time.

The Court goes on to say, "He used a knife..." It is only Melanie's word that Paul had a knife. She had a knife, as evidenced by photos taken of her bed by authorities on June 2, 2006. No other knife was ever found anywhere that could be proven to be the knife she alleged Paul had that day.

The Court, moments later, says "...and breaks into the victim's house in the middle of the night and she wakes up with a fellow with a knife on her..." Again there is no proof Paul broke into the house or had a knife. It is only what she alleged.

Judge Damon rambles on about "protecting the public," "rehabilitation being iffy," and "the safety of the community," and accepts the recommendations of the district attorney for sentencing, even though the Pre-Sentencing Investigation report done by the state's own appointed investigator recommends a much less-severe sentence.

Court of Appeals Document No. 2009AP1059-CR, the Appellant's Brief and Appendix submitted on Paul's behalf by his appellate attorney, John A Birdsall, is a document which is an appeal from Judgement of Conviction and an Order Denying Post-conviction Motion. It lists John A. Damon as the judge. To understand the significance of this document, the reader needs to know that if a convicted person appeals his/her conviction, the appeal is presented to a Court of Appeals which then rules on whether the appeals will be considered. If the Court of Appeals rules that the appeals should be considered, the case is then returned to the judge who initially presided at the original trial and imposed the sentence given. In Paul's case, his appeal was denied at the Court of Appeals level.

A brief explanation of the issues of what the Court of Appeals is being asked to review by Attorney Birdsall in the Appellant's Brief, cited above, includes that while Paul did receive a hearing (back at the Post-conviction Court level), it was only a partial hearing and did not address all the claims Paul had made.

In the court system, there is a special kind of hearing referred to as a Machner Hearing. This can be asked for through a motion to the original trial court if the appellant (Paul, in this case), feels that he was not given proper representation by his trial attorney, called ineffectual assistance of counsel. Under the guidelines of the Machner Hearing, the trial attorney must make an appearance before the original trial judge to be questioned as to whether he/she had followed the accepted procedures in preparing to defend the client. Without going into all the details, Paul was trying to show that his court-appointed attorney, Lester Liptak, had not done the necessary things to give Paul the best possible representation. Attorney Birdsall (the appellant attorney for Paul) had asked for a Machner Hearing, which subsequently did not actually happen. Judge Damon had excused Attorney Liptak from appearing to be questioned in a Machner Hearing as to how he had prepared for Paul's trial.

Three other points that Paul appealed included how Judge Damon handled things during the sentencing hearing referred to above. Did the trial court punish Paul for asserting his right to a jury trial and to confront witnesses against him? Did the sentencing court unduly defer to the State (represented by the District Attorney) in imposing the sentence? Was the sentence excessive?

The Table of Contents from the Appeals Document lists the main arguments that Attorney Birdsall presented to the Court of Appeals as to why the Post-conviction Court had erred in several ways in dealing with Paul's case. These are that the postconviction court had erred in: denying Paul a hearing on his claim that trial counsel Liptak failed to object to the introduction of impermissible hearsay and prejudicial "other acts" evidence; denying Paul a hearing on his claim that trial counsel had no reasonable theory of defense and failed to impeach Melanie Miller with prior inconsistent testimony offered at the preliminary hearing; exercising sentencing discretion, in punishing Paul for going to trial, in uncritically adopting the State's recommendation and analysis, and because the sentence is excessive and cruel.

In a concluding Statement on Oral Arguments and Publication, Mr. Birdsall briefly described the process beginning with the original criminal complaint filed against Paul on June 2, 2006.

After a Preliminary Hearing (June 16, 2006), a two-day trial was held on March 29-30, 2007. The jury returned verdicts of guilty on four of six charges, and not guilty on a fifth one. The judge found him guilty on the sixth charge. Paul was sentenced on July 27, 2007, to a total of 24 years in prison followed by 13 years of extended supervision. Paul was 39 when he was arrested in 2006; he will be 63 if released after 24 years in prison, and 73 after the supervision ends. In essence, it could be said that he received a life sentence.

Paul filed a postconviction motion alleging that he was entitled to a new trial based on a claim of ineffectual assistance of counsel, and a claim that he was entitled to have his sentence vacated and remanded to a new sentencing hearing. After additional briefing, and a partial Machner Hearing on February 24, 2009, the circuit court filed an order, dated March 2, 2009, denying defendant's motion for postconviction relief.

A letter to Judge John Damon, dated February 20, 2009, from Paul's appellant attorney, John Birdsall, refers to an enclosed affidavit of Greg Martin in support of Paul's motion for postconviction relief as explained above. Greg Martin had been hired by Birdsall as an expert witness on behalf of Paul following Paul's conviction.

This affidavit was filed with the Clerk of Pierce County Court as a supplement to previous briefings filed on Paul's part. A particular portion of this affidavit relates to Paul's claim for ineffectual assistance of counsel regarding trial counsel's failure to request or conduct forensic testing of the physical evidence admitted at trial. Greg Martin is an expert in forensic science, having served as a City of Madison (Wisconsin) Police Officer for thirty years, five of which were with the Identification Section as a crime scene investigator and as a forensic professional.

The letter goes on to enumerate the various responsibilities Martin had in that capacity, including photo lab work, evidence collection processing and handling, fingerprint development and performing comparisons. Furthermore, Martin was involved in numerous investigations of major crimes and testified in court on many occasions regarding his finds as an expert witness.

Additional responsibilities "encompassed processing crime scenes and evidence, which included document-

ation, collection and processing items of varied nature."
According to the affidavit, Martin "employed different
elements of forensic technology, including forensic light
sources, tool mark comparisons, tire impressions and
numerous other forms of forensic comparisons."

The letter goes on to describe other credentials Martin
has to qualify him as an expert witness, and that, since
retiring from active police service, he has testified in many
counties in Wisconsin as to his expert opinion involving
criminal evidence.

In the affidavit enclosed with the above referenced
letter to Damon, there are five forensic opinions that
Martin presented "to a reasonable degree of scientific
certainty regarding the physical evidence admitted into
evidence" during Paul's trial.

In Martin's opinion:

    a. "there is no evidence that a person stood on the
hood of the Durango prior to the time that the
photo in Exhibit #5 was taken;

    b. "neither the filet knife listed as Exhibit #49, nor
the Buck brand knife with a green handle owned
by the defendant, were used to cut the wire ties
in Exhibit #23 and #47;

    c. "the ends of the tapes for Exhibits #45 (from...the
garage) and #50 (from the...bedroom) do not
appear to match. The piece of duct tape from
Exhibit #50 is not from the roll found in the...
vehicle, Exhibit #25;

    d. "all the Exhibits that contain duct tape would
likely have latent fingerprints suitable for
comparison and/or DNA samples suitable for
analysis;

    e. "a 6 foot person could not have suspended themselves above the floor and therefore hung themselves from the 8 foot high rafters in the...garage using the rope found in the rafter of the...garage in Exhibit #46 as photographed."

As an explanation for the importance of these five opinions, they offer "substantive evidence that had forensic testing/crime scene analysis been performed by trial counsel, the result in this case would have been different."

Paul had explicitly requested that counsel conduct forensic testing and scene analysis in support of his defense. None were performed.

The letter goes on to detail further arguments that would have supported and strengthened Paul's defense and would demonstrate that much of the state's case would have been put in serious doubt and led to an acquittal.

Had the Machner Hearing been held as scheduled on February 24, 2009, six witnesses would have been called to testify to their knowledge of certain issues that were relevant at the trial and in the appeal. None of these witnesses had been contacted by Paul's counsel prior to his trial. The guidelines from the American Bar Association "demand a duty to investigate and to explore all avenues leading to facts relevant to the merits of the case." In Paul's instance, he had requested counsel to interview and take statements from the six witnesses referred to above.

In the final statement in this letter from Birdsall to Damon, Birdsall says, "The defendant will call trial counsel Lester Liptak to testify about his preparation for this trial and his decisions and 'strategies' in conducting the trial."

As indicated earlier, the Machner Hearing never occurred, and Lester Liptak never was required to appear before The Court to testify. At an abbreviated hearing, DA John O'Boyle spent time questioning Mr. Martin's credentials as an expert witness, and much of what Martin would have testified about his findings were never allowed to be presented, a further instance of Paul's civil rights being violated.

In the decision from the Court of Appeals (District III), dated and filed March 9, 2010, Paul's appeal was denied, although this Court did affirm that the circuit (trial) court had "erroneously exercised its sentencing discretion."

This "erroneous action" on the part of the circuit court is contained in that court's denying Paul's postconviction motion regarding the Machner Hearing as stated in Judge Damon's comment at the end of the abbreviated hearing. He said, "I don't find anything that's been presented…would have required an attorney to present any of this evidence (Martin's findings) that would have made any difference at trial…compared to all the other evidence that was presented…Even if I accept everything in the brief, I don't find it was prejudicial by anything that was done to make a case that there was ineffective assistance. So I agree… (with the prosecutor) for all the reasons he stated…"

The Judge is making an assumption as to how the jury might have determined things with the additional evidence and testimony that could have been presented to them for their consideration at trial.

Following the denial by the District III Court of Appeals, Paul's appellate attorney, Birdsall, prepared and submitted an appeal to the State Appellate Court to have his case reviewed. Four reasons were given in the request for review:

1. "This court should grant review to address Krauss's claim that he was punished for going to trial. Because the issue raises 'a real and significant question of federal or state Constitutional law,' and the Court of Appeals Decision 'is in conflict with controlling opinions of the United States Supreme Court.'

2. "Review is warranted because the Circuit Court's failure to provide sufficient reasons for imposing consecutive sentences presents real and significant federal and state Constitutional questions, and because this Court should consider establishing, clarifying, and applying its considered doctrine to this recurring question.

3. "Review is warranted because the Court of Appeals' holding herein that '*Allen* does not require a written decision when a court orally sets forth its reasoning' cannot be found in *Allen*, or any other published decision of this Court or the Court of Appeals.

4. "Review is warranted to clarify whether the failure of the Circuit Court and the Court of Appeals to address several of Krauss's postconviction claims conflicts with *Allen*."

It should be noted that Paul's Petition for Review was dated April 8, 2010. This request was refused by the Wisconsin State Supreme Court in the response from the State Assistant Attorney General Mark A. Neuser, dated April 9, 2010.

To pursue an appeal further, that is, to the U.S. Supreme Court, would have required additional monetary cost to retain John Birdsall in the range of at least $50,000. Mr. Birdsall explained to us that very few actual cases make it to the Supreme Court for review, and having exhausted our financial resources, Paul's case was never submitted to the Supreme Court for consideration.

A final example of Birdsall's efforts to address the violation of Paul's civil rights can be seen in an email sent Aug. 30, 2008, to me, Paul's mother, from John Birdsall in which he acknowledges that the appellate process is quite confusing, and that "basically we need to get back and have a meaningful Machner Hearing with Liptak actually testifying."

Anytime a case is appealed, it is sent back to the court that handled it in the first place. The same judge and same prosecutor will be in place for any review or new case that might occur. It is our opinion that "pride" may cause these court officials to turn down a review so as not to "tarnish" their reputations as competent and trustworthy representatives of the legal system.

Issue 2: Ineffectual Assistance of Counsel

While Issue 1: Violation of Civil Rights is a complete point on its own, it overlaps to a certain degree with Issue 2: Ineffectual Assistance of Counsel, as shown by some of the ideas explained above. However, there are additional documents in Paul's case file that are more specific to Issue 2 starting with a letter dated August 8, 2006, from Paul to the Public Defender Office in Hudson, Wisconsin.

When a defendant cannot afford to hire an attorney, the State is obligated to provide one under the *Miranda Rights*. At one of Paul's pre-trial hearings, his court-appointed attorney, Kerry Lemke Kelm, had requested a change of judges from the Pierce County District Judge Robert Wing and for a Speedy Trial. After being granted that request, Ms. Lemke Kelm immediately left the courtroom and went to the Clerk of Court's office to request that she be allowed to withdraw from Paul's case. His original trial date had been previously set for mid-September 2006. This would have allowed only about one month for a new attorney to prepare Paul's defense.

In a letter he was told to write to the Hudson, Wisconsin, public defender office, he states that his first attorney is the one who initiated the action asking to be removed from the case. Paul's letter requests that a substitution be made for the public defender (Lemke Kelm), and explains that she had asked to be allowed to withdraw. Paul, also, mentions that he understands this can only be done once, and that no further substitution can be requested.

This point is important as, later on, Paul was accused of asking to remove her. This letter from Paul becomes significant when the second appointed attorney also asked to be allowed to withdraw.

With the change of judge request from Paul's first attorney having been done, Paul had been appointed a second attorney, William Lamb. In a letter, dated December 26, 2006, to John Damon, Trempealeau County District Judge, Paul expresses his concerns that Lamb has not consulted with him since being appointed in September.

At a hearing with Mr. Lamb as his attorney, the date for Paul's trial also had been reset to mid-February to allow Lamb time to prepare Paul's defense. Paul's letter to Damon addresses what has gone on since these several changes had occurred. It further describes Lamb's failure to use the intervening months from September to actually meet with Paul and do his preparations.

Because these concerns were never addressed by court

officials, I took it upon myself to contact the Wisconsin State Public Defender Office in Madison. After I spoke several times to Deborah Smith, Director, Assigned Counsel Division, and forwarded a copy of Paul's Dec. 26 letter to the Judge to her, she then sent a letter, dated Dec. 28, 2006, to Mr. Lamb in which she reminds him that, "Most attorneys do accept collect calls in order to maintain adequate contact with clients in jail."

She goes on to say, "It is important that attorneys keep their clients reasonably informed of the status of their cases. It sounds like it will be important in this case to keep a good record of those contacts."

This letter clearly reprimands Mr. Lamb for failing to do the very basic things to properly prepare to defend his client, Paul.

In a hearing held in September 2006, Paul was forced to give up his right to speedy trial because his newest public defender needed time to prepare for his trial. A new trial date was set for mid-February 2007, giving his attorney about five months to prepare.

By the time Paul received a letter, dated Jan. 25, 2007, from Attorney Lester Liptak, Paul had been moved from the Pierce County Jail in Ellsworth to the Pepin County Jail in Durand. This is often done with inmates awaiting trial if a particular jail is getting overcrowded.

In this letter, it is clear that once again another newly-appointed attorney, Lester Liptak, is now representing Paul, his third one. It is also clear that, once again, Paul's trial has been postponed, this time to the end of March. His new attorney now has about two months to prepare, and it seems, is doing his duty.

Paul faxed eight letters to Liptak between March 10 and May 29, 2007, spanning the time just before Paul's trial, through the time of his trial, and following the trial, after Paul had been convicted of five of the six charges that had been brought against him. Based on what could be called "Lawyer 101" requirements for any attorney to prepare to represent a client to the best ability, it would seem that Paul's contention is that his lawyer, Mr. Liptak did not do what he needed to do, thus affirming that Paul had the basis for the Machner Hearing, referred to under Issue 1, above, that he had requested and been denied during the appellate process which started in February 2009.

Issue 3. Arranged/Falsified/Misrepresented/ Untested Evidence

Issue 3 will address how items such as photos, plastic zip ties, a kitchen knife found at the scene, duct tape, green rope and others were presented, identified, and handled by officers in the collection process, as well as in their testimony at trial regarding them.

On Day One of Paul's trial, various photos identified as having been taken by several different officers at the "crime scene," were entered as exhibits by District Attorney John O'Boyle. Two of them show what appears to be a small wooden table with what looks like a short piece of silver duct tape hanging off the edge. Although Melanie, the "victim," had said that Paul had placed duct tape over her mouth, she had testified that he had done so while they were out in the garage, that he had removed it in the garage, and they had never returned to her bedroom that day.

Attorney Liptak asked Officer Todd Hines, "So when they left her bedroom…, she never told you ever that they ever came back into the bedroom, did she?"

Hines replied, "No."

Officer Hines has been testifying in response to questions from Mr. Liptak. He affirms that Melanie told him she and Paul never returned to the bedroom after Paul had allegedly taken her out to the attached garage earlier that morning. This is an important point, as the next questions pertain to the piece of duct tape recovered by investigators from the night stand beside Melanie's bed.

Liptak asks, "The duct tape that had been used to cover her mouth allegedly and it was removed in the garage, you never saw that, did you, in the garage?

Hines answers, "I don't remember. It's not in the photographs that I took."

Liptak: "If you would have saw it, you would have photographed that?"

Hines: "I took brief photographs; investigators took a complete set of photographs as well."

The photos taken by police officers at the scene in the bedroom clearly show a piece of tape on her bedside stand. This piece of tape was later removed by one of the officers, and placed on a piece of paper. It was never subjected to any kind of testing to affirm whether or not either her DNA or Paul's might have been on it. Testing could have answered some questions about her credibility in the allegations she made against Paul. This tape was not entered as evidence during the trial.

Several photos taken from different angles show a green rope tied to garage rafters; some of these also show the hood of a Dodge Durango where the accuser alleged Paul stood to tie rope and try to "hang" himself.

O'Boyle asks Hines to describe what each of the photos depicts.

Officer Hines says, "I think once we had photographed

it the way it originally was, I believe one of the investigators...did pull it down."

This and other photos of the rope are important for several reasons. First, it would seem that the rope was not hanging down when first viewed, which seems to suggest it was not tied on the rafter by Paul at the time his accuser alleges. Secondly, one of the officers possibly tampered with the rope to make it appear that it was hanging down all the time.

One of the photos shows a close-up of a knot in the rope, which in a second photo appears to be at about the same height as a shelf above the vehicle. In still a third photo, the end of the rope is shown near the tire of the vehicle, indicating the length of the rope from the rafter to the floor.

Two other views show a roll of tape and a short piece of rope on what appears to be the hood of a vehicle. Incidental to showing the roll of tape, it can be noted that there are no footprints or dents in the hood of the vehicle. Melanie claimed Paul stood on the hood to tie the rope. If Paul had actually done that, a reasonable person would expect that at the very least there would be dusty footprints, and probably some indication that a person of Paul's weight would have left some kind of mark on the hood.

In his Supplemental Report, dated 6/5/06, Investigator Wade Strain refers to various pieces of evidence he observed and collected from the scene. He states that he took photos of items that a second officer, Bruce VonHaden, collected. After taking these photos, he says, they went inside and took additional photos, including those of a knife located on the bed, and some duct tape from her bedstand.

This would appear to be the same duct tape Hines was asked about at trial. Hines also testified that "when we found that knife the investigators were there and had moved the bed covers around and found it."

Strain also reported that he was the one who removed the rope from the garage, which he says "was tied in a noose type fashion." A photo of the rope shows a small loop at one point in it. It would be difficult to describe the loop as a "noose type" as it appears far too small to fit over a person's head.

Strain mentions that he took photos of marks on Melanie's wrists that "did appear to be of the same dimension as the zip ties collected." There is no mention or record of any measurements being made of the "noose," the length of the rope hanging from the rafter, or the marks on her wrists.

Officer Strain testified in court and was questioned by Attorney Liptak regarding what he did, observed and photographed at the scene. Strain took responsibility for the various photos that were introduced into evidence.

Strain describes finding a knife on the bed lying in plain sight. It will be noted that in photos, it appears that the knife was at least partially covered by the quilt on the bed, and may not actually have been "lying in plain sight," suggesting that someone pulled back the top edge of the quilt to display the knife.

In testifying about the marks he says he observed and photographed on her wrists, Strain never mentions taking any kind of measurements. Nor does he say he did any measurements of the zip ties found or of the rope from the garage.

After being asked if the "noose was open wide enough to put over your head," Strain replies, "No," and then refers to it as a "loop."

On day two of the trial, Melanie was called to testify by O'Boyle. She fails to indicate where the rope was originally that "he pulls down." Furthermore, it is not clear how there were all the pieces of rope that O'Boyle asks about. His questions that continue about the rope are, again, not clear.

O'Boyle asks Melanie about Paul allegedly getting on the hood of the Durango.

O'Boyle asks "And then at that point you said he got onto the hood of your Durango?

Melanie: "Yes."

O'Boyle: "Did he jump on the hood?"

Melanie: "Hopped on there" then adds, "He just hopped up on there, like he might have put one foot on the wheel..." Melanie tells O'Boyle that Paul was wearing white "tennies."

O'Boyle then goes on to say, "He was moving around and fiddling with the rope that he had tossed over the rafter, correct?"

There is no place in her testimony here where Melanie has described what O'Boyle just said happened.

O'Boyle again leads Melanie to say yes when he says, "Now, at that point he made a loop in the rope, correct? – And he put a loop over his head or around his neck, is that correct?" Continuing, O'Boyle says, "A loop or noose I guess. Then you say that he stepped off the side or the front of the hood, correct?'

Melanie replies, "Off the side."

O'Boyle now asks, "Off the side. And you say that he hung there for a few minutes, correct?"

Melanie: "No, more like a couple of seconds."

O'Boyle asks, "And was he showing any signs of

choking?"

Melanie: "His eyes got big and his face got red real quick."

O'Boyle: "Now, he took the rope off his neck?"

Melanie: "Yes."

O'Boyle: "Cut the noose off his neck, correct?"

Melanie: "I don't think he cut it off. I think he loosened it and pulled it off. I don't remember him cutting it off."

O'Boyle also asked Melanie about the duct tape as to when it was put on her mouth. She answered that it was put on in the garage. O'Boyle then refers to the ties Melanie claimed were put on her wrists, and uses the term "clipped" in referring to how the ties were removed.

This term is important because the expert witness, Greg Martin, would have testified that the ties he examined were cut with a two-bladed cutting tool, yet there is never any mention of Paul having or using such a tool. Melanie only mentions a knife in all her testimony and statements.

Melanie is asked about the two knives she said Paul had had. O'Boyle refers to "that knife," and to Melanie having said Paul had it in his pocket. O'Boyle then asks if "he had both knives with him when you went into the garage area." She says, "I believe so."

The only two knives that are ever referred to in all testimony and statements are the knife belonging to Melanie found on her bed by Strain and other officers, and the "green-handled knife" she claimed Paul had with him. Three photos taken by officers show a knife lying on her bed that she identified as belonging to her. Other testimony by Melanie also affirmed that after leaving the garage she and Paul never returned to the bedroom.

The "green-handled" knife, which was never found

anywhere in her house or Paul's vehicle, and indeed, was actually discovered sometime after Paul's arrest in an unlocked gun cabinet in his rental house in Ellsworth to which he never returned after June 2, 2006. This is the knife that Greg Martin examined during the appeals portion of Paul's case.

Prior to August 21, 2007, Jean and Rolland Krauss met with Lt. Dennis Sorenson, Pierce County Sheriff's Department, regarding return of Paul's cell phone. The phone, which was never listed in any Replies from the District Attorney, as required by law to Motions for Discovery by any appointed attorney, was never introduced as evidence at any time. Jean wrote a letter to Sorenson reiterating what had been discussed at the meeting, including the fact that Sorenson had talked to someone on the phone in their presence regarding the possibility of things being deleted from the phone. During that meeting, and in the letter, we seriously objected to anything being deleted. Sorenson had told the person he was talking to that the phone should be retained with all information as possible evidence for the defense, and in the possible appeals process.

In a letter, dated 9/2/2007 from Sorenson in reply to Jean and Rolland regarding disposition and handling of the cell phone by VonHaden, we were told that access to the phone at some future time would only be with permission from the DA and/or the court.

Issue 4: False and Contradictory Statements by Accuser/Law Enforcement Officers

Melanie's handwritten complaint, dated May 31, 2006, raises several questions that should have caused the police authorities to wonder about her honesty. On her statement, Melanie recorded her cell phone number, and writes about having to purchase a new cell phone and to secure a new phone number because of "Paul calling her." At first thought, this may not seem important, but it becomes significant when on subsequent statements Melanie writes, starting on June 2, 2006, she continues to record the same cell phone number as on the May 31 complaint.

To help the reader understand the importance of this fact is that, later, Melanie also claimed that Paul continued to call her on that same number AFTER he was in jail. My question is how would Paul have her supposedly NEW cell phone number after he is locked up?

Either she really didn't ever get a new phone number, as she claimed back on May 31, or she somehow gave her new number to Paul between June 2 and June 7. This would have been the time between her 911 call to the Pierce County Sheriff's office on June 2, and the time when Paul was actually arrested on the basis of her allegations about what she claimed happened on June 2.

Considering Melanie's past history that I have already hinted at in describing how she did not seem to be totally committed to being in a relationship with Paul since they first met back in March 2003, and the discrepancy regarding her claimed need to get a new cell phone number, a reasonable person might have questions about how reliable Melanie might be.

It should be noted that it is on this particular statement that she reveals that she called him in April 2006 about items of his still at her house. She says, "We talked for a bit and before I knew it he came over. We were intimate 5 times the beginning of April."

Her next statement, dated June 2, 2006, is Melanie's

account of what she alleges happened in the early morning hours of Friday, June 2, 2006, but mentions nothing about any "sexual abuse" having taken place.

Once again, she has written the same cell phone number that she wrote on the May 31 report she filled out for police authorities. Is this her "new" number of her "old" one? If it is her new one, how would Paul have been able to call her (as she claims he did) unless she gave him the new number sometime between May 31 and June 7, the date Paul was arrested.

She alleges that he called her several times between June 2 and June 7, 2006. Phone records for her "old" cell phone number show that it remained an active number until fall 2006.

At first reading, her June 2 account would seem very condemning to Paul, until a reasonable person visualizes the details of the "scene" and "actions" she describes. Furthermore, if this initial report of what she alleges happened is compared to several other accounts she later gave, including her testimony during Paul's trial, there are some obvious discrepancies, omissions, and additions among and between them which again would raise questions about her allegations.

When trying to compare this version to her other accounts, things become problematic, starting with attempting to plot out the contradictory timelines she gives in these various accounts of what she claims happened that morning between 5 a.m. and 9 a.m.

On a television program entitled, "Cold Justice," Kelly Siefer, one of the investigators, comments, "When a suspect changes his/her story, it indicates he/she is lying." It would seem the same thing applies to anyone else involved in a criminal case. An additional comment from that same program says, "Truth is the truth, anything else is lying."

From June 2 to June 7, 2006, I did not have any contact with Paul, even though I called his cell phone several times. It was only much later that I learned some of what was happening with him in those five days. Since I do not have firsthand knowledge about where he was and what he was doing, I will not try to relate anything about those days in this account. The next thing I can relate is when we learned that Paul had been arrested in Wabasha, a small town south of Red Wing, about 40 miles from Ellsworth.

From documents that eventually became part of Paul's case file, I know that Paul was taken to the police department in Wabasha. An arrest warrant for him had been issued on June 2, when officers were unable to locate him following Melanie's 911 call earlier that day.

In her Domestic Abuse Victim Worksheet, dated 6/2/06 – There are several things to note:

- First, she again has given the same cell phone number as on May 31, where she had said she had to purchase a new cell phone with a new number;
- Secondly, she now adds more "details" to the "abuse," circling "pushed, shoved, threw objects, pulled hair, sexually abused, attempted to suffocate, attempted strangulation, bit." Most of the items she circled were not mentioned in her original statement from that day;
- Third, she says she is suffering pain, but goes on to note that she refused to see a doctor or to be transported to a medical facility to be examined. If she was so "abused" alleging she had been pushed down a stairway, and had red "marks" and bruises, why did she refuse medical

attention? Also, no rape kit was ever done on her, and no "evidence" was tested for possible DNA, either hers, Paul's or any other person's. She also indicates that no property was damaged;

- Fourth, she states that none of her children witnessed the "abuse";
- Fifth, she says that Paul was arrested before for abuse once with her. She does not give any date as to when that allegedly happened. If she is referring to the incident on March 1, 2006, Paul was not actually arrested at that time. He was stopped by Red Wing police, and by Pierce County Sheriff's deputies, and transported to Mendota Mental facility where he was released; and
- Sixth, she again states there were no witnesses to the "abuse."

On Trial Day One, Paul's first wife, Becky (Rebecka Langer) related what Melanie supposedly told her had happened on 6/2/06. Becky specifically says Melanie did not mention anything about sexual assault, even though Melanie "was hysterical" throughout the ten minute phone conversation. Becky says that Melanie said Paul had put duct tape over her mouth, yet Becky also says that Melanie claimed she had said, "I can't help you, I'm tied up..." when Melanie says Paul "...went to hang himself."

When O'Boyle asked, "Did she give – tell you anything else?"

Becky replies, "...and swung himself onto the Durango and got himself unhooked and they talked and she got him calmed down or whatever and she said he left."

In his cross examination of Becky, Liptak asked, "Did she mention sexual assault to you?"

Becky replies, "No."

Another witness that testified in court was Jodi Weinkes, a woman Paul had been phone/text/email friends with for some years prior to meeting Melanie. On Trial Day One, Jodi testified that in a phone call with Paul on June 2, not only did he not say he had held a knife on Melanie, but that Paul told her "That's what they're saying" or "That's what she's saying I did..."

A bit later in her testimony, Jodi says, "He said that she (Melanie) had said he held her at knife point..."

These statements of Jodi's were in response to Liptak's question, "Now, did he just come flat out and say that hey, I held a knife on my wife?"

Jodi: "No."

Liptak: "How did he characterize it?"

Jodi: "Well, the first conversation, like I said, he didn't say, 'I held her at knife point.' He said

"Held her at knife point," but then later on we were talking and I said so, you know, what –what happened and he said...that she had said he held her at knife point..."

On Trial Day 2, Savannah Wickman, 10-year-old daughter of Melanie, testified that her mother told her "what had happened to her." She also affirms that when she was interviewed by Investigator VonHaden (on June 7, 2006) she had actually started her comments to him with "...my mother woke up with Paul's hand on her mouth."

This statement by Savannah, and recorded on a video of her interview with VonHaden, clearly shows that Melanie had told Savannah "what happened" long before Paul's trial. Anything that Savannah then testified to in the June 7 interview, and in court, may be tainted by what she had been previously told by her mother.

Liptak asked Savannah, "And during that time your mom told you what had happened to her, correct?"

Savannah replied, "Yeah."

Liptak then asked, "And she went through the whole thing with you, didn't she?"

"Yeah."

"And, in fact when you started your interview with Investigator VonHaden and he asked you to talk about what happened that morning, the first thing you said was my mother woke up with Paul's hand on her mouth. Isn't that what you said, do you recall?"

"Yeah."

"So everything you were about to tell him at that point is what your mother had told you, wasn't it?"

Savannah replied, "I don't understand the question." When Mr. Liptak repeated it, she answered, "Yeah."

In Melanie's testimony on Day Two of the trial in March 2007, she hedges about telling Savannah about "what happened." Melanie does not appear to be telling the complete truth about what she told Savannah or when she told her.

A recording of the interview in Paul's case file from June 7, 2006, verifies that Savannah first started telling what Melanie had told her about "what happened."

When Melanie was being cross examined on day two of the trial, Liptak asked about conversations she had with Savannah about what happened June 2. He says, "Savannah wasn't interviewed until June 7th, isn't that correct?"

Melanie replies, "Yes."

"And you were interviewed the day before, on June 6th, isn't that correct?'

"I believe so."

"During the time from June 2nd to June 7th, you didn't discuss this matter at all with your daughter—your daughter?"

"Well, we had some conversations about it. She was scared."

"I may have."

In questions from O'Boyle, Melanie testified regarding getting a restraining order against Paul in early March 2006 at about the same time she filed for divorce. He asked her, "From March 9th (the date of the injunction), did the two of you have any type of contact at all?"

Melanie says, "Yes."

"What type of contact?"

She replied, "There may have been a phone call or two."

"Were there attempts to reconcile at all in that period in March?"

"Not in March."

"Okay. How about in April?"

"April, yes."

"Okay. And the attempts to reconcile in April, who initiated those?"

"I made a phone call to him initially."

"And why did you do that if you had filed for divorce and you had an injunction?"

"I missed him."

"Why did you miss him?"

"I was lonely." She also admits that she had once previously filed for divorce, but that the marriage was not entirely bad. She says they were together intimately five times during April 2006, four times at her house and once at his. Her comment that she was "in fear" seems to be another instance of contradictory comments/actions on her part.

O'Boyle asked her, "...Why did you think that?"

"He was a scary man."

"At times?"

"At times."

"Other times he wasn't a scary man?"

"Other times he was great."

As she continued her testimony, Melanie was asked about saving "angry" messages that she alleged were from Paul. At some point, she talks about buying a recorder and re-recording these phone messages, which were never tested for authenticity as to whose voice was on them. Officers' reports indicate the accuser re-recorded her re-recordings on a disc, and sent it to them and/or the District Attorney. She referred to some of the recorded messages being received on May 30, one day prior to her statement, dated May 31, where she said she had to purchase a new phone and number.

O'Boyle asked, "Your cell phone have I'm assuming voice mail capability?"

"Yes."

"When you received messages, would you delete those messages right away?

She replies, "If they didn't – if they weren't angry messages, I deleted them."

"Okay. Angry messages, did you save them?"

"Yes."

"Why did you save them?"

"Once again, I thought I was going to need them for something."

She testifies that prior to May 31, she did not contact anyone from the sheriff's department about them. When asked why she contacted them then.

O'Boyle asked her, "Did you – were you in fear at all when you were getting those messages?"

"I was nervous."

Moments later, she is asked why she didn't report those earlier messages, and she responds that she "was embarrassed."

During her testimony she claimed she twice "checked" that every door was locked, except the outside garage service door, and pointed it out on a diagram of the floor plan of the split-level house. She also described a "smaller knife, a dark green handle," and another knife, which she admitted was hers that she had on her night stand for "protection."

In Melanie's testimony she described the alleged "sexual" contact, the alleged conversation at the time, and how it "stopped" when she told Paul he would have to "rape" her.

Summation

As has been already stated, the above documents referred to are all in Paul's case file. There are many more examples from that file that illustrate the four issues I have addressed in Part 2, Paul's Key: Violation of Civil Rights; Ineffectual Assistance of Counsel; Arranged/Falsi-fied/Misrepresented/Untested Evidence; and False and Contradictory Statements by the Accuser and Law Enforcement Officers. I have included these particular ones because they clearly demonstrate how the entire "justice" system dealt with Paul in this "he said-she said" situation. In a comment made to Paul in the aftermath of everything, it was suggested that if he had been able to retain his own attorney from the beginning, and not have to rely on a Public Defender as he did, he would likely never have even gone to trial. The anguish and loss that resulted from this whole ordeal, and indeed, this book, would never have happened. Two young boys would not have suffered the heartache and separation they have endured. How different all of our lives would have been. Only God knows that.

Addendum

In my efforts to present a significant and effective argument that justifies why Paul's case should be reopened for further in-depth study, I researched various related topics on the internet. The references I have made here are not part of the official court or legal records in Paul's case file.

In addition, over the time Paul has been incarcerated, we have prepared various appeals to the public, legal authorities, and media to draw attention to the miscarriage of justice we feel prevailed in Paul's case starting when he was arrested and continuing through the entire process to the present day. These will be discussed and explained for consideration as to how a concerned person might conclude that justice was not served in Paul's case. I feel these are pertinent for clarification and to inform the reader about the background and significance of the issues raised in Part 2 above.

Paul wrote the following, and similar, letters to various media personnel in his efforts to prompt someone (Paul's Key) to come forward and champion his cause:

To Whom It May Concern:

My mother, Jean Krauss, can tell you that the former District Attorney, John O'Boyle, of Pierce County (WI) where my case was prosecuted, seems to display some unethical behavior in several ways. She has compared DA John O'Boyle to DA Kenneth Kratz of Calumet County who was "sexting" to a woman whose husband he was prosecuting. My reason for writing to you is very simple. My loved ones and I need your help. I truly believe that after hearing our whole story, you will not want to rest until our plight is over. I will thank you in advance for anything and everything you do for us.

My intent is not to convince you of my innocence in this letter, but to raise questions about how my case was handled that led to my wrongful conviction. It would take a *War and Peace* length book to list all of the proof we have, and to fully understand the whole story. What we are asking is that you be our voice for justice. Ever since this nightmare started for us, we have sought that one person, that one voice that would bring light to this terrible, horrible miscarriage of justice. We truly believe you are that voice. Please be that voice for me and my family. Included with this letter are examples of some of our attempts to bring my wrongful conviction to an end. Every attempt has brought the same result: our District Attorney and his "good ol' boy club" thwarting our efforts.

From the moment I was arrested in another state, I had my right to counsel denied, not once, but twice, and was brought back to Wisconsin without an extradition hearing. Two Public Defenders withdrew prior to trial, and my trial was one-sided because my third Public Defender simply did not prepare or present any defense. I was sentenced to what the District Attorney John O'Boyle asked for and received verbatim from the Judge (Honorable John Damon of Trempealeau County). All my appeals attempts were tossed aside without any case law being cited. After a few of my letters (limited to 300 words each) to the editor of our weekly hometown newspaper were published, and I was banned from submitting any additional letters, the District Attorney submitted, and had published, his 450+ word version of my case. We feel that this man may be responsible *for my being banned from submitting more letters due to the fact that his letter appeared the very week that I was notified that no more of my letters would be accepted for publication.*

We sent a letter to some of my jurors and received a written response from one of them. The response includes "Christian" talk, but certainly no "Christian" walk. In my letter, I mentioned James 4:17 ("Anyone, then, who knows the good he ought to do and doesn't do it, sins.") The juror simply ignores everything because of his pride in not wanting to admit he and the eleven other jurors were wrong, seems a bit ironic. Another juror came to talk with my parents and expressed some of the same misgivings in regard to how my defense attorney mishandled my case.

My mother sent a letter to our new Circuit Court Judge (Honorable Joseph Boles). Copies of her letter were forwarded by Judge Boles to the district attorney and the presiding judge. It should be noted that neither the District Attorney nor the presiding Judge acted on Judge Boles' having forwarded copies to them.

Because there is such a large amount of paperwork in my case file, there is no way that we can send you copies of all the police statements, "victim" statements (yes, there are multiple versions from her), court documents, affidavits, photos, and other documents that we have that more than prove my innocence. What we are asking is that you or an associate of yours would meet with my mother at her home and look at the entire file that she has in her possession. I must mention that once you or your associate look at my case file, you will likely respond in the same way that others have who have seen it by wanting to climb the highest mountain and scream at the top of your lungs, "This man is innocent!"

I don't know if you have read <u>Actual Innocence</u> *by Barry Scheck, Peter Neufeld, and Jim Dwyer, but I would ask that you do so because my story and that of my family over the past 6 years would fit right in the pages of that book. As with Dennis Fritz, Ron Williamson, Walter Snyder, and others whose stories are told, our story could be included in many chapters of the book because of all the wrong perpetrated on us.*

Several pages in the book tell of Edith Snyder, mother of Walter, and her tireless pursuit of justice for her son. Let me tell you, she has nothing on my mom. For 6 years my mom has basically devoted her life to getting justice for us, in addition to raising my two sons, Dylan, almost 19, and Austin, 16. My parents sold the family home and land that they had owned for 43 years, and which had been in my father's family since being homesteaded in the mid-1860's. Many of their possessions and some of mine were auctioned off at the time of the sale in order to hire an appeals attorney, who turned out to be just another "big-shot," big talk, no results, high priced lawyer. After my case was turned down at the Appellate Court level and then at the State Supreme Court level, he said he could only submit it to the Federal Supreme Court if he was paid an additional $50-100,000, Because that money was not available, his help was not available either, in spite of his having claimed he truly believed in my innocence.

My parents have sacrificed their retirement years. When they should be living out the rest of their days in relative carefree style, they are left to raise my sons, whose mother (not the 'victim') basically tossed them out two years ago. That is a whole other chapter in this horrible story. My parents spend considerable money for my phone calls, visits to see me, paying for supporting my sons, and supporting me with purchases I cannot get for myself. If it were not for my mom, my sons and I would be up the proverbial creek without a paddle. If for no other reason than to let her enjoy the rest of her retirement years, please help us. She can be reached by email (october40jean@yahoo.com).

As we have said right along, everything we claim can be proven by simply looking at the documents we have. The prosecutorial misconduct, police cover-up, false statements, and blatant lies on the stand can all be proven. As shown in Actual Innocence, the prosecution's 'out' is the so-called "harmless error" catch-all. They are untouchable and can't be held liable for any wrongdoing or part they may have played in the wrongful conviction of innocent person – in this case, ME! For an innocent person, like me, the two most dangerous words in the language of the law are "harmless error." Their errors are harmless to everyone except the defendant and his/her loved ones, who suffer the sentences just as much as the wrongfully convicted. The 'harmless errors' are what our District Attorney blithely calls 'unavoidable collateral damage'.

Before I close this letter, I would like to share with you some quotes from some famous people. I'd like you to consider them while putting yourself in my place or the place of my loved ones. As you read them, ask yourself how you would feel if no one seemed to care enough to come to your aid.

"Injustice anywhere is a threat to justice everywhere." - Martin Luther King, Jr.

That is such a powerful statement that it was used on his memorial in Washington, DC. Are they just words carved on stone, or do they mean something, and therefore need to be acted on?

"The thing is, you don't have many suspects who are

innocent of a crime. That's contradictory. If a person is innocent of crime, then he is not a suspect." - Edwin Mease, Attorney General of the USA, 1986.

The police said they did not look for anyone but me because the "victim" said I did it, and her motives for lying were never investigated. There was another man with her there the night before, but she was never taken to the hospital to have a rape kit done, in spite of the fact that she was claiming sexual assault. What was she afraid they might discover? I was convicted on her word and her word alone.

"(A district attorney) may prosecute with earnestness and vigor – indeed he should do so. But, while he may strike hard blows, he is not at liberty to strike foul ones. It is as much his duty to refrain from improper methods calculated to produce a wrongful conviction as it is to use every legitimate means to bring about a just one." - Justice George Sutherland for the majority, Berger v. United States 1935

The tactics used by the DA in my case, even before it went to trial, are criminal in the least. I have a letter he wrote on Pierce County letterhead to Judge James Duvall in Pepin County regarding a small claims civil action I had legally obtained against the "victim." In addition, I have enclosed letters (Exhibit #7) that she wrote to the courts. It seems that while she expressed "fear" of being in the same courtroom with me for the civil action, she had no fear of being in the same courtroom for the divorce proceedings she had brought against me. Because of the letters written by the DA and her, my civil action was dismissed without my having any chance to speak out in the court about it, thus, again violating my civil rights.

The DA had also previously refused to bring contempt of court charges against the "victim" after she had violated court orders in our temporary divorce decree which mandated that she not move her residence without notifying the court and me, not remove anything from the marital house, and that she keep up the mortgage payments on the house. However, she did move (out of state, in fact) without notification, did remove items, and did not keep up the payments, which resulted in the house going into foreclosure. All while I was in custody. The DA's blatant disregard for my rights, as well as the law and moral and ethical issues, is unbelievable.

I would also like to mention the fact that the DA and the "victim" are on each other's Facebook pages. Chris Rickert of The Milwaukee Journal, reported on Ken Kratz of Calumet County (WI,) and his texting ("sexting") to women whose male significant others he had prosecuted for domestic abuse cases. Calumet County citizens were outraged. As my mother suggested, you might want to check into the Pierce County (WI) DA who seems to have either accepted or issued an invitation to be 'friended' by the 'victim' whose ex-husband (me) he had prosecuted, and for whom he had secured a 24 year sentence based on her word alone. My mother has printouts to document this, should it have been removed.

Many people, when hearing about my case and extreme sentence, ask me one of two questions: "What did you do to the DA?" to which I answer, "Nothing!" Or, "What is the connection between/what's going on with the DA and the 'victim' (my ex-wife)?" I don't really have an answer for that because I don't know, but it is of interest to note that her sister was often at the courthouse in connection with her job in the title industry while working at the same title office where my ex-wife worked at the time.

A final quote I wish to include sums up my entire "defense"

representation that I had at my first court appearance:

"We set our sights on the embarrassing target of mediocrity. I guess that means about halfway. And that raises a question, Are we willing to put up with halfway justice? To my way of thinking, one-half justice must mean one-half injustice, and one half-injustice is no justice at all."
- Harold Clarke, Chief Justice of the Georgia Supreme Court.

This was my biggest hindrance from the start, but especially during my trial as reflected in the comments in the juror's response letter, but particularly in the documented actions and inaction of my three different court-appointed attorneys who did not even follow basic procedures in handling my case.

When I had a court-ordered Pre-Sentencing Investigation (PSI) done through a private service, the man doing the investigation, who is a 35+ year veteran of the Wisconsin Department of Corrections in many functions, including probation officer, in the first words out of his mouth after doing all the paperwork, documents, statements, etc., said, "You know, if you'd have had your own paid attorney, we wouldn't be having this conversation?" That was and still is a pretty hard pill to swallow. It means that if I could have hired my own attorney, I never would have been convicted, according to this veteran of the "system." It also implies that if you have the money to hire your own attorney, and not have to rely on the "appointed" attorney guaranteed by the Miranda Act, you probably won't be convicted when you are actually innocent. In my case, even the Miranda Act was violated when I was twice refused an attorney because I 'couldn't afford one anyway', according to the statement of the investigator, following my arrest in June 2006.

I apologize that this letter had gotten so long, but I felt I had to give you enough to convince you to do something about my situation. All it will take is for you or one of your associates to go to my parents' home in Ellsworth (WI) and look at all they have in my case file. We have nothing to hide, unlike the DA who refuses to release my cell phone and/or the information, text messages, and pictures on it. My mother is more than willing to let you examine the file and she would welcome you into their home to do so. We are available for interviews, either in person or by phone. I'm not sure the prosecution would be so welcoming.

My two sons made a video on YouTube in which they talk about how their lives have been affected by this ordeal. I am enclosing the most recent photograph of my sons and I, taken on December 31, 2012, so that we become real people to you, not just names in a letter that would be too easy to ignore.

I will close by asking a simple favor of you, please help us. Look at what we have, and decide on the side of justice. Know that you are in my thoughts and prayers, and I look forward, soon, to sitting down with you as a free man, to be interviewed. Again, thank you for taking the time to consider my urgent request. Hebrews 13:3

Sincerely, Paul Krauss

A photo of Paul and his two sons was attached here in the original letter.

An article published on November 8, 2013, by The Associated Press, which I printed off the Internet, carries the headline, "Former prosecutor gets jail for wrongful conviction." The person referred to, Ken Anderson, a former Texas prosecutor, had won a conviction that sent an innocent man to prison for nearly 25 years. He had been accused of tampering with evidence in the 1987 murder trial of Michael Morton. Morton was released in 2011 after DNA evidence showed he did not beat his wife to death as accused.

The ironic thing is that Anderson "agreed" to serve ten days in jail, complete 500 hours of community service, to be disbarred, and was fined $500. Anderson had previously apologized to Morton, referring to "failures in the system," but maintained there was no misconduct. Following the 1987 conviction, Anderson had gone one to spend eleven years as a state judge. He resigned that position in September 2013.

Judge Kelly G. Moore commented, "In a case like this, sometimes it's hard to say what meets the ends of justice and what doesn't. There is no way that anything we can do here today can resolve the tragedy that occurred in these matters." Morton has been instrumental in pushing through the Michael Morton Act, which helps compel prosecutors to share files with defense attorneys that can help defendants' cases.

The television program *Inside Edition* carried a story on January 18, 2014, titled, "False Rape Accusations Catch Up With Accuser." James Grissom spent ten years in prison after being convicted of raping a mother of two, Sara Ylen in 2001. She had identified him from a photo in police files.

Ylen wrote about her experience as an alleged rape victim in an inspirational book, "Treasures of Darkness" in which she called Grissom "the man who destroyed...my life." She also compared herself to the television character Xena, The Warrior Princess for courageously "reliving every grisly, lurid detail" of the attack at Grissom's trial. Her story was also featured on *Captured* on the Oxygen network.

Prosecutors have since discovered that her story of

rape was a lie. They learned that she had made numerous false rape accusations against as many as nine other men. Furthermore, she claimed to be suffering from terminal cancer, receiving hundreds of thousands of dollars for medical services. She falsified medical records, including X-rays to show bone marrow cancer,
And even underwent chemotherapy.
An explanation of why she might tell such lies was offered by Dr. Gail Saltz a psychiatrist that appeared on *Inside Edition*. She said, "There are people who feel that they are victims, and need to be victims and need to be put up on a pedestal as suffering but soldiering through."

She has been found guilty of making a false report of a felony and tampering with evidence in Port Huron, Michigan, court. Grissom, who served ten years and has now been exonerated, rape charges dropped, commented, "She just totally destroyed my life."

The question remains, was Paul falsely accused of the charges brought against him based solely on the accuser's unsubstantiated allegations?

Additional documents from several online sources reflect on the various issues in the above pages. For example, while researching "legal definition of attorney misconduct," I learned that the Model Rules of Professional Conduct were adopted by the American Bar Association (ABA) in 1983. These had been modified several times since their origins in 1908. The model rules have been used by 40 states to create official guidelines for professional conduct; 11 states or jurisdictions have continued to base their ethical codes on the earlier model; California has developed its own rules. Whatever their basis, the codes/rules define the lawyer's proper role and relationship to the client. "It is essential that lawyers understand the ethical codes under which they must operate. Failure to do so may result in not only disciplinary action by the relevant professional authorities but also suits against the lawyer."

I printed the information out and mailed it to Paul. He then read through the pages, highlighting those particular parts under Rule 8.4 that he felt pertained to either or both his trial defense attorney and the prosecuting district attorney. In illustrating what we feel could be construed as attorney misconduct on the part of the two attorneys, I include the following excerpts on attorney misconduct from Rule 8.4:

"It is professional misconduct for a lawyer to:...

(c) Engage in conduct involving dishonesty...deceit or misrepresentation;

(d) Engage in conduct that is prejudicial to the administration of justice

(e) State or imply an ability to influence improperly a government agency or official:

(f) Knowingly assist a judge or judicial officer in conduct that is a violation of applicable rules of judicial conduct or other law."

The information I found emphasizes that trust "is a defining element of the legal profession, and without it, the practice of law could not exist." The model states that, "An attorney will be guilty of misconduct, for example, if she or he fails to provide competent representation to a client with diligence and promptness regarding a client's legal concerns, or to keep a client informed of legal proceedings."

The ABA has recognized sexual relations between attorney and their clients as a significant ethical problem for the legal profession. This "may involve unfair exploitation of the lawyer's fiduciary (trust) position and presents a significant danger that the lawyer's ability to represent the client adequately may be impaired..."

Included, also, are these statements:

"Any breach of the trust by the attorney that underlies the relationship between the attorney and the client can be considered misconduct."

"Ethical rules also govern the conduct of attorneys before courts. Thus, an attorney is guilty of misconduct toward the court if he or she brings a frivolous, or unnecessary, proceeding to court; makes false statements to the court; offers false evidence; or unlawfully obstructs another party's access to evidence."

"Lawyers have also been found guilty of misconduct with regard to the advertising of their services...if that advertising is false, deceptive, or misleading, makes unsubstantiated comparisons to another lawyer's services, or proposes means contrary to rules of professional conduct, the attorney can be charged with misconduct."

Several examples of misconduct that may be drawn from court documents and Paul's case file, have already been referenced previously in this book. I would like to add a couple more. On her Facebook page, printed 2/6/2015, under Melanie's Friends list, the name of John M. O'Boyle is included.

On his Facebook page I printed that same date are the following posts from John M. O'Boyle –

"Why is it that guys with a bunch of bad-ass looking tattoos turn into blubbering piles of goo when bad mo-jo is about to befall them in a courtroom?"

The response posted by Melanie Augustine (her fourth married name) reads: "Always gonna be my hero!!!" followed by the smile emoji.

Both of these comments were actually posted between March 7 (2012) at 4:02 pm and March 7 (2012) at 5:03 pm. Following his defeat for election as Circuit Court judge of Pierce County in 2010, Mr. O'Boyle completed his term as district attorney. He then ran for re-election to that office, which he had held for about 20 years, and was defeated. He then opened his own private law practice in January 2013. His LinkedIn page verifies his education as College of St. Thomas, 1982-1985, Bachelor's degree; William Mitchell College of Law, 1985-1989; attorney from September 1989-January 1993 with Davison and Vlack Law Office; from January 1993-December 2012 as District Attorney, State of Wisconsin; and his self-employment from January 2013-Present.

Mr. O'Boyle created a website to advertise his private law practice in which he made certain statements that seem somewhat confusing and questionable. One example is repeated several times on different pages of his website. "For more than 25 years, I have been handling criminal cases in St. Croix County." Since he served as DA in Pierce County 20 years, by his own admission, had worked at the Davison-Vlack Office 4 years, and had only gone into private practice in 2013, he could not have handled criminal cases in St. Croix County 25 years unless he had worked in Pierce County as DA and in St. Croix County simultaneously?

He specifically mentions that his office "represents clients throughout St. Croix County as well as college students at the University of Wisconsin-River Falls and the University of Wisconsin-Stout. Another comment made on his website states that he "will get you the best possible resolution of your criminal charges so you can move on with your life." His list of types of cases says that he has "successfully handled everything from misdemeanors to felony charges, including... domestic violence and sex crimes."

On page after page of his website, O'Boyle continues to make statements that contradict the way he handled Paul's case. On the page advertising "Sex Crimes Attorney" in particular, he says, "Everyone is innocent until proven guilty. However, sex crime allegations can destroy family and personal relationships, end careers and irreparably damage your reputation...I fight sex crime charges, and work hard to protect my clients' freedom, their families and their reputation." This from the person who called what happened to Paul's family "unavoidable collateral damage."

He goes on to say, "When you are facing criminal sex charges, you are facing the full force of the government. As a former district attorney, I know the steps prosecutors will take to build a case against you and 'prove' your guilt. Drawing on this inside knowledge, I build strong, solid criminal defense strategies that undermine the prosecution's case and get my clients the best possible resolution of their criminal charges."

A couple more statements I include here come from O'Boyle's page labeled, "Domestic Violence Lawyer" where he says, "Alleged victims often no longer want to file charges after the dust has settled. Unfortunately, once police are involved, prosecutors will often refuse to dismiss charges."

He goes on to say, "I thoroughly investigate claims of domestic violence for weaknesses in the case. I interview witnesses, and look at the history of the alleged 'victim' to uncover evidence of emotional instability and identify any motive he or she have for making false claims against you."

Mr. O'Boyle subsequently was hired as an assistant district attorney in a county north of both Pierce and St. Croix Counties in Wisconsin. His webpages are no longer available for reviewing, although I have the pages I originally printed out in full.

I offer the thoughts and ideas presented throughout this book to the reader for consideration. Is there reasonable doubt that Paul's case was severely mishandled during this entire sequence of events lived by Paul and his family? Can this wrong be corrected? Are you "Paul's Key" to answering these questions and getting the justice we all deserve?

About the Author

Jean is a former junior high school English teacher who lives in Hudson, Wisconsin, with her cat Diablo. She is the mother of three adult children and grandmother to three handsome grandsons and four beautiful granddaughters, all young adults.

www.ingramcontent.com/pod-product-compliance
Lightning Source LLC
Chambersburg PA
CBHW050528280326
41933CB00011B/1505